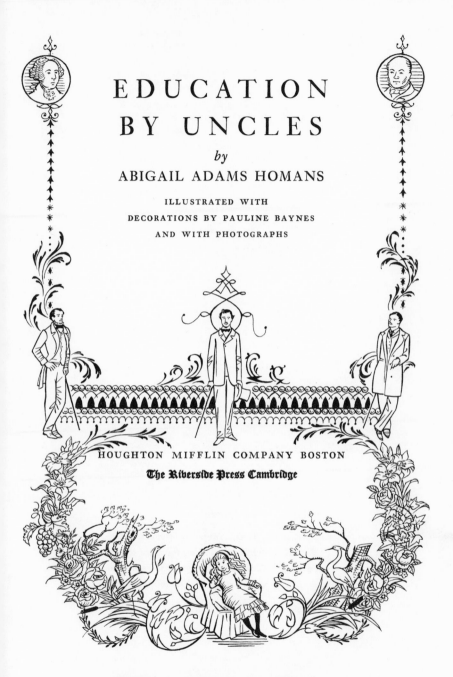

EDUCATION
BY UNCLES

by

ABIGAIL ADAMS HOMANS

ILLUSTRATED WITH
DECORATIONS BY PAULINE BAYNES
AND WITH PHOTOGRAPHS

HOUGHTON MIFFLIN COMPANY BOSTON
The Riverside Press Cambridge

To my son
George Caspar Homans

ILLUSTRATIONS
following page 86

"An architectural anomaly" — the house of Mrs. Homans's
father, John Adams, on Mt. Wollaston

The Old House in Quincy, Massachusetts, became
Brooks Adams's permanent home

The garden of the Old House showing the library

Charles Francis Adams at Harvard

John Adams about the time of his graduation
from Harvard in 1853

Henry Adams at the time of his graduation
from Harvard in 1858

Brooks Adams while he was in school in England
in the 1860's

Brooks Adams at Harvard (1866–70)

Abigail Adams in about 1895

Surrenden Dering, the manor house in Kent where Abigail
Adams visited her Uncle Henry in the summer of 1898

Part of the "complicated caravanserai" at Surrenden Dering

The Glades in Minot, Massachusetts —
"monumental relic of a past age"

Henry Adams from a drawing by John Briggs Potter

EDUCATION BY UNCLES

CHAPTER ONE

W HEN I SPEAK of my background I am speaking of
something that is as dead as the Dodo. The Quincy
that I knew in my childhood now lives only in memory —
a quiet country town, with little relation to the present
bustling, suburban city. Quite properly, the old town has
been submerged by the flood of enterprise and energy that
have made Quincy the important center it is today, and the
few landmarks of the past that are left have become his-

I

toric ghosts — preserved for posterity through the kindness and interest of historical and antiquarian societies.
The Quincy Historical Society and the Daughters of the
American Revolution look after the two simple old farm-
houses lying at the foot of Penn's Hill where John Adams
and his sons lived. The lovely old Dorothy Quincy house,
now below street level on the road to Boston, is cared for
by the Colonial Dames, and what is now rather pompously
called the Adams Mansion, and which our generation of
Adamses always referred to quite simply as the Old House,
has been taken over by the federal government and is
beautifully kept up by the Department of the Interior.

Of all the relics the only one that preserves its original
use is the splendid stone church that dominates the center
of the city. Built of Quincy granite, it guards under its
stern portico the remains of the town's two Presidents, and
their sepulcher makes a fine example of New England aus-
terity at its stark and vigorous best. They lie, the two old
statesmen, with their wives beside them in a solid stone
crypt under the portal of the church. Their sarcophagi
are of granite too, as hard, uncompromising and grim as
they were themselves. They wait there as the tablet in the
church above them reads — "till the last trump shall sound"
— and they wait in great dignity.

It is a wonderful coincidence that John should have died
on the fiftieth anniversary of the signing of the Declaration
of Independence, saying with his last breath, "Thomas
Jefferson still survives," and that Jefferson had died only

a few hours earlier in his own Monticello. Together·they had labored over the Declaration of Independence, and it was fittingly dramatic that they should both die on its fiftieth anniversary. Jefferson and Adams represented different schools of thought, but fundamentally they respected and admired each other, and though at times violent political enemies, with retirement from public life the differences vanished, the old ties were renewed, and there is no more touching correspondence than that between the two old friends through their later years. What more incomparable tribute could Jefferson have paid to Adams than to say of him, "disinterested as the Being that made him."

John Adams's son, John Quincy, added a dramatic touch to his own end, when, having returned after his presidency to the House of Representatives in Washington as a delegate from his Quincy district, he collapsed at his seat when rising to address the House. His last words were: "This is the last of earth — I am content." He died as he would have wanted to — in harness. John Quincy's son, the first Charles Francis Adams, was the father of Louisa, John Quincy, Charles Francis, Jr., Henry, Arthur, who died as a child, Mary and Brooks. Of this brood, my father was John Quincy Adams, and he as well as other members of that generation will appear throughout these memoirs.

As the town of Quincy has changed, my father's place at Mt. Wollaston has been completely obliterated, and it is only with the greatest difficulty that I can trace any of the landmarks of my childhood, vividly though I can see them

3

in my mind's eye. The modern bulldozer has done its deadly work on the none too salient features of our gentle slopes, and streets and houses cover the big hayfields where I used to ride. Gone too are the gravel pits that made such sheltered playgrounds on cold windy days, while even the salt creeks where my father used to take me to fish for smelts on frosty autumn mornings have mysteriously vanished — swallowed up by the expansive demands of industry.

Fishing for smelts could be cold work for a small girl, so when my feet became thoroughly congealed my father would put me ashore at Germantown where the creek ran into Quincy Bay and let me run up to the "Sailor's Snug Harbor" where I was looked after by a delightful inmate, Mr. Jones. The Sailor's Snug Harbor was a private charity run for the benefit of American-born sailors of the Merchant Marine who might be dependent in their old age. At the time of my childhood there were so few American-born seamen left to enjoy such benefits that Mr. Jones lived in great comfort. He used to thaw me out in front of the huge kitchen range and fill me up with the strongest and hottest of black coffee — which would, almost instantly, send me off into a profound sleep in which I would remain, dead to the world, until picked up later by my father. In warmer weather, Mr. Jones taught me to row and also explained to me the rudiments of looking after a boat properly. In fact my childhood had a distinctly salty flavor, for in full view from our house, across an estuary called Black's Creek, was another Sailor's Home, a dreary federal institution where old navy seamen lived. It had none of the charm of the Snug Harbor and was considered a blot on the landscape.

My father's land began just east of the Mt. Wollaston Cemetery, which lay about a mile from the center of Quincy on the road to Hough's Neck (pronounced Huff's). Some of his land has now been incorporated into the cemetery while the rest has gone for land development. Right through the middle of it now runs Route 3A — one of the main routes from Boston to the South Shore. The road bridges Black's Creek, destroying in its progress the old willow trees that used to shade our broken-down bathhouses. To the east our land ran down to the Germantown woods — a lovely section of big oak trees full of anemones and lady slippers in the springtime.

Most of the place had been included in the original John Quincy farm — John being of the third generation of the Quincy family from Edmund, the emigrant. A worn farmhouse shaded by a fine line of linden trees still stood there when my father built his cow barns nearby, and it was from that farm that John Adams with his eleven-year-old son, John Quincy, left in the February of 1778 to join the frigate *Boston* lying out in the Bay, which was to try to run the British blockade and take him to France as a Peace Commissioner. It must have been an anxious time for John, who knew the danger, but exciting for the boy for all that he was torn at leaving his mother behind. When I lived at

5

Mount Wollaston the setting was exactly the same and our farm road wandered down to the beach precisely as it had on that cold February day in 1778.

Our house stood on a gentle rise that overlooked Boston Bay and the islands in the harbor, and above it was a pleasant little hill made famous as the scene of the Maypole set up by Thomas Morton and his roistering followers. Morton was a satellite of a certain Captain Wollaston who had established a trading post in the neighborhood and then left to seek further and more profitable adventures. When Wollaston moved on, Morton remained behind and proceeded to make trouble. He called himself "Lord of Misrule" and corrupted the natives with his convivial practices. It is from him that the place got the name of "Merry Mount," for all that he spelled it "Mare Mount," or "Mount by the Sea," for the benefit of his more pious neighbors to the south. That deception, however, was of no avail, for when the news of his shenanigans reached Plymouth, Myles Standish came up on the double with eight stalwart soldiers and put a summary stop to such goings on. But it was the indignant and sanctimonious Governor Endecott who, on his arrival at Salem a few months later, did Standish one better by crossing the Bay and having the offending Maypole leveled. He even tried to wipe out the memory of the Maypole by changing the name from Mare Mount to Dagon's Mount, but there he overstepped himself, for Dagon's Mount had no significance, so the little hill was always called colloquially by the old

name of Merry Mount. My father himself, being of a convivial turn of mind, wanted, when he built his house there,
to continue to call his place Merry Mount, but Puritan
prejudices still lingered and he compromised on the more
conventional name of Mount Wollaston.

Originally the whole hill had been bare of trees, it being
one of those terminal moraines, composed mostly of gravel,
that were deposited in the ice age to plague the farmer of
the future. Still there was one notable exception to the general barrenness, for a single weather-beaten cedar tree had
clung for unknown years to the northern slope of Mt.
Wollaston. This tree was such a well-known landmark
that it was later incorporated in the seal of the City of
Quincy which shows the summit of Mt. Wollaston with
the lone cedar clinging to its side and the sea behind as a
background. Below is the Latin motto *Manet* — "It remains." In my childhood the tree still stood, a grim but
dignified skeleton wreathed in woodbine and sheltered by
the young pines that were growing up around it. In the
savage northeaster of November 1898, which sank the
steamer *Portland* and which is still referred to as the Portland storm, the old tree met its fate. My family preserved
its trunk for many years in the cellar of our stable, but it
has long since found a more fitting resting place among the
Quincy memorabilia. The spot where it once stood is
marked by a modest stone. To me as a child the old tree
was out of bounds, since beyond it one's doings were concealed from the house.

My father as a young man still lived in the Old House during his father's absence as Minister to England, and planted trees over the bare slopes, so that eventually the hill lost its Maypole character, except for a bare strip along the top where either no trees would grow or where perhaps my father out of sentiment never planted any. My father loved trees and besides planting from seeds he transplanted a quantity of young stock — not only oaks, maples and elms that were indigenous to that hard soil, but beeches, spruces and larches — which, with pines to protect them, eventually made a lovely park. The beeches particularly were his pets and they well repaid his care, for many of them have survived even through the ruthless process of modern development.

My father's house was placed just below the north-eastern crest of Mt. Wollaston and has, mercifully, been long since demolished. It was a dreadful house, an architectural anomaly, built in 1877 and '78 at the worst period of domestic construction. As the view was to the north and east the preposterous and pretentious house had also to be oriented in that direction, and to make matters even worse the pleasant southwesterly exposure was ruined by a massive stone tower embedded in the corner of the house in that favored quarter. This horror effectively cut off all southwest summer breezes as well as the longed-for winter sun. The house was further shadowed by a huge piazza which enclosed it on the northern side. No ray of sun ever penetrated the parlor behind it, with the result that it was never used. That parlor was a prize package, a truly amazing room furnished with a complete set of ebonized sofas and chairs upholstered in red velvet with gilded lions' heads emerging at odd corners. On the floor was a straw carpet covered in summer by a really beautiful Aubusson rug, which was replaced in winter by a red Turkey one in the firm belief of my parents that red was a cheerful color and would make you think that you felt warm even when you knew better. From long experience in Quincy I have never taken much stock in the influence of color. The interior of our stone tower was a high dismal hall with insufficient lighting and practically no heating facilities. As Theodore Roosevelt would say, "it was about as easy to heat as a bird cage." What heat there was came from a single hot-air register, and the trick of managing that was to stand over it until one's skirt billowed out warmly and then rush for the nearest chair to conserve as long as possible the cherished heat. This dreary hall was lighted by a ponderous chandelier which hung from the ceiling (three stories up) to the level of the second floor, an atrocious swaying monstrosity that had to be lighted from the ground, which feat needed both finesse and great strength, as one long pole had to find and turn on the gas cock while another stick bore the lighted taper. As no maid could or would do it, my poor mother always struggled with the horrid contraption while stoutly maintaining that it was all perfectly convenient.

Naturally it was many years before the full peculiarities of the house dawned on me, for like all children I felt that as it was mine it must be perfect, but with time the house came into its true perspective, and I now glory to remember it as the ugliest and most inconvenient house that I ever was in. Any landscape gardening outside was practically nonexistent. A few flower beds were scattered around, and hideous stone urns with a few hardy annuals in them bordered our avenue. In the autumn we boasted a bed of red salvias chosen again for their supposed ability to cheer up the dying season. We had some fine lilac bushes rescued from Abigail Adams's garden at Penn's Hill and two lovely wisteria vines that wreathed our granite porch and were a softening touch to the bare New England surroundings. Mercifully we did not pass many winters at Quincy. We moved to Boston as regularly as clockwork right after Thanksgiving and returned as near the first of May as possible — but at times when the family felt hard up we stayed in Quincy, and those winters were certainly daisies.

CHAPTER TWO

T HOUGH MY FATHER'S place at Mt. Wollaston lives only in my memory, the family house on Adams Street has survived almost intact, complete with some of the family pictures, most of the china and all of the furniture, a curious jumble of federal and diplomatic debris. The house stands unpretentiously beside the highway protected by its stone wall which gives some privacy to its lawns and garden. John Adams's name for it of "Peacefields" was singularly appropriate, but curiously enough the name never stuck; perhaps it sounded too ostentatious for the Quincy of that era, for to future generations it was known quite simply as the "Old House" — quite as though there were no other old houses in the neighborhood. Commonplace as the name may be, the house itself is utterly delightful. It started as a small farmhouse on the estate of a gentleman called Vassall who used the place as a country retreat from the gaieties of Boston. Vassall was an enterprising man who also owned property in the West Indies, and conceived the quaint idea of paneling his simple little parlor in Quincy with Santo Domingo mahogany. It gave the house a touch of elegance for all that it made the parlor a trifle gloomy in winter. John Adams — the vandal — couldn't stand it when he came to live there, and had the walls painted white, but later generations restored them to their own lovely color. The Vassall family were loyalists and left the house to its fate when they fled to England at the outbreak of the Revolution — and it was there, when John Adams was in London in 1787, that he had an opportunity to buy the property from a Vassall heir. John and Abigail had always liked the place and were delighted to get it, as they had long outgrown the primitive farmhouse at the foot of Penn's Hill where they had lived during their early married years. There is a very human legend about Abigail and the house — on first seeing it on her return from England after an absence of four years, she sat down on the front steps and burst into tears, the reality being so much smaller and more insignificant than she had remembered it. The story adds that John was so distressed by this outburst — for Abigail was not given to tears — that to appease her he promised to add to the house so that she might have a proper room in which to display her French furniture, salvaged from the house in which the Adamses had lived at Auteuil while John was stationed in France collaborating with Dr. Franklin and Mr. Jefferson in negotiating several commercial treaties. Perhaps it was memories of the huge Auteuil house surrounded by gardens which so distressed Abigail when she first saw her future home in Quincy after her long absence abroad. It took John some years to fulfill his promise, but in the end he was as good as his word, making a handsome addition to the eastern side of the house which not only gave Abigail her parlor but himself a most spacious study above.

The house has been added to several times since John's first effort, but it has always been done with fundamental good taste, so that the exterior has not suffered, although the interior is a curious jumble of makeshift closets and passages which add a certain interest to the long history of its expansions and adaptations to meet the needs of a changing society.

Immediately to the west of the house is a formal garden subdivided by paths bordered by hedges of box. The box has never flourished in the hard New England climate, but at least it has survived, and the garden has remained intact throughout the years thanks to the plan that John

Adams drew up for it and that has been carefully preserved. It still boasts the York rose that Abigail brought home with her from some English garden to brighten her home in the New World.

At the northwest corner of the house stands the Stone Library built by the first Charles F. Adams, my grandfather, in which to preserve the family books and papers that were overflowing his study. It was built of solid Quincy granite, but it was not fireproof, and a few years later the more valuable manuscripts and papers had to be removed to Boston to insure their safekeeping. That left the library still lined with ancient books but otherwise only a lovely peaceful refuge for old or young, work or play. The library consists of one lofty rectangular room, roofed by a vaulted ceiling and lighted by several long windows reaching to the ground beyond which can be seen the hollyhocks and delphiniums bordering the garden paths. The harsh granite of its outer walls drips with wisteria in the spring and is red with the turning woodbine in the autumn. Its furnishing consisted of a huge table down the center of the room, a few dilapidated leather chairs that the Interior Department has now renovated, some family busts and relics and a small full-length portrait of John Adams looking his plumpest and most pompous. The library is a delicious sanctuary on long summer afternoons, cool, quiet and shaded. It has another attraction particularly for the young, and that is an open gallery that circles the upper reaches of the book-lined walls enabling the would-be scholar to inspect the otherwise inaccessible higher levels. To mount to the gallery you used a shaky little ladder which was so easily detachable that one could either maroon an enemy up there or else, by bad luck, be marooned oneself. The books made a nice wall covering but they had little interest for us of the younger generation as they were mostly in Latin and had no amusing pictures — our interests at best were far from literary. To our credit, be it said that we did surprisingly little material damage for all our irresponsible tendencies, and although we rummaged through all the drawers and closets, as far as I can remember we put everything back when we were through with it; being allowed perfect freedom, we seem to have respected it.

Of my grandfather, Charles Francis Adams, I have only the vaguest memory, for he died when I was still very young. There is only one little episode which impressed itself on me and that was when I was taken up to see him one autumn afternoon. He was sitting — a feeble old man — by the fire in the middle front bedroom. He seemed to know me for he said, "So this is Abigail" — a

personal touch that I never forgot. Of my grandmother I have no recollection, although she outlived
her husband by several years. On family visits I always
managed to escape from the grown-ups to the more congenial society of a delightful maid named Rosa who, after
feeding me adequately, would let me play in her private
apartment where a most lurid lithograph of Mt. Etna in
violent eruption gave me never-ending thrills of "delicious terror." With my grandfather's death in 1889, the
Old House was left unoccupied. Soon, however, Uncle
Brooks took it over as his permanent home, when he was
married in the September of that year.

My grandmother was born a Brooks of Medford and inherited considerable wealth from her father, Peter C.
Brooks, a prominent merchant. She was a worrier by nature, which trait she may have handed down in the form
of that self-distrust so evident in her two younger sons,
Henry and Brooks. My father, John, was the oldest son,
but there was an older daughter, Louisa Catherine — called
Lou — as well as a younger one, senior to Brooks, who was
the baby of the family. Lou I never saw, but she is im-
mortalized in my memory by her classic remark always
quoted with pleasure by her brothers, that "she would
marry a blackamoor to get away from Quincy." She ac-
tually married a severe and bearded gentleman from Phila-
delphia, named Charles Kuhn who, I presume, served her
purpose, for they lived in Italy which was gratifyingly far
removed from Quincy; she died there childless after an ac-

cident in 1870. Lou must have been a remarkable woman, for all her brothers were devotedly attached to her — one of the few subjects on which they could all wholeheartedly agree. She was not beautiful but she had style, self-confidence and wit and was evidently very charming, for she was invariably spoken of as a *femme fatale*.

Between my father and his brother Charles, a short two years his junior, there was always a very close and affectionate relationship. They even looked alike — short, stocky, broad-shouldered and in later years, of course, completely bald. Graduating with the Harvard Class of 1856, Charles, without any marked predilection for the law, selected it as a suitable profession for his active and inquiring mind. Unwilling to spend further years of intellectual drudgery at Harvard, he started reading law in a private office but the advent of the Civil War soon distracted him, and by 1861 he had entered the army, leaving it four and a half years later as Colonel of the First Massachusetts Cavalry. He was married soon after the end of the war to a charming New York lady, Miss Mary Ogden (Aunt Minnie), and took a year's vacation in Europe to recover his health, somewhat shattered by his army service. At home once more, he found that he could not face the intolerable anticlimax of a law office after his war experiences, and with his insatiable energy at once looked around for some more congenial calling. He spotted the railroads as the greatest developing force in the country and proceeded without delay to familiarize himself with their problems, and the abuses to which they were prey. In collaboration with his brother Henry he began writing articles for the monthly magazines, hoping to stir up public opinion for adequate legislation to control the depredations of the railroad magnates. Between them, the two produced some first-rate propaganda, and, undeterred by public apathy, Uncle Charles worked and wrote incessantly until in 1869 his efforts were rewarded when the Massachusetts legislature passed an act creating a Board of Railroad Commissioners. He was then appointed one of the three members. For ten years he worked as a Railroad Commissioner and then refused renomination and became successively Chairman of the Board of Arbitration of the Trunk Lines and afterwards President of the Union Pacific. That assignment lasted for six bitter years, until, to his great relief, he was removed by Jay Gould and thrown back to begin his life over again.

Nothing daunted, Uncle Charles took to his pen once more and became the historian of his native Quincy and the adjacent countryside, as well as a versatile and aggressive writer on an extraordinary number of unrelated subjects. He used to say that he suffered from an inferiority complex, but I knew him as one of the most self-confident and combative of men, loving to stir up discussion and reveling in criticism. He worked unremittingly with my father on the town affairs of Quincy, helping to produce what subsequently was known as the Quincy system in the public schools as well as being instrumental while a Park

Commissioner in saving for the people of Massachusetts the Blue Hill reservation and the Middlesex Fells. His body was as vigorous as his mind; he rode every day of his life — usually before breakfast — and he loved the sea, being a keen swimmer as well as a competent yachtsman. At our summer playground, the Glades Club at North Scituate, no northeaster could stop him from taking his daily swim — and I can still see him as he used to stand on a cold September morning gazing out at a gray sea while pensively rubbing his bald head and happily murmuring; "My God, how dreary!" He had built himself a house at the top of President's Hill in Quincy where he and his family lived for many years until his restless energy asserted itself once more and he pulled up stakes and moved to Lincoln. To me he was always a sympathetic and well-loved figure.

Uncle Henry — the next Uncle — escaped from Quincy early in life, when, as a young man just out of Harvard, he went to London for eight years as secretary to his father, Charles Francis Adams, who was American Minister to England. Then within two years of his return, he accepted an invitation from President Eliot to become Professor of Medieval History at Harvard. In 1872 he married Miss Marian Hooper whose brother was the Treasurer of the college and settled down in Boston, with a summer home at Beverly Farms. Uncle Henry was a natural teacher and made a great mark for himself while he was at Harvard, but his heart was not in the work, Boston was socially uncongenial, he was restless, and by the late seventies he had resigned, moved to Washington and begun his life-work as a historian and biographer. He took little interest in the Old House at Quincy and although he came back later, after the death of his wife, to pass some summer months there, it was only to use it as a quiet haven where, with access to the family papers, he could work in peace on his *History of the United States*. It was there in the Stone Library that I remember him when I was a little girl.

He always had with him his two Skye terriers, Marquis and Possum, lying dutifully at his feet, and was himself a vision of neatness in his white linen suits which gave an alien touch to the conservative Quincy scene. His papers were never in disorder and when he wrote, it was most beautifully done in his large careful handwriting. He was not ruffled or annoyed at our approach, and I never remember seeing Uncle Henry in a temper — indeed, he said that a temper fit gave him a bilious attack — but his two brothers, Charles and Brooks, could produce, when provoked, quite appalling ones. Uncle Henry's visits to Quincy were never scheduled; he came and went equally unexpectedly, and before one had become used to having him there, he would disappear as mysteriously as he had come. Somewhere in the years before my father's death in 1894 Uncle Henry had got into my father's bad graces by committing what was for my father the inexcusable solecism of refusing to accept an honorary degree from Harvard College. It was not so much the refusal but the way in which it was done that aroused my easygoing, though at times inflexible, parent. At the time of that Commencement Uncle Henry was staying right in Cambridge at the house of his brother-in-law, Edward Hooper, who was the Treasurer of the College, but instead of pleading illness or asking to be excused, he simply remained quietly at home and let the degree go by default. It was perhaps natural; Uncle Henry was desperately shy and self-conscious and probably honestly felt that his *History* did not merit the reward, which feeling, combined with his own nervous reaction, made the situation intolerable to him. For whatever reason, he could not face it and stayed away. My father, on the other hand, who was then a member of the Harvard Corporation, felt that his brother had not only slighted his own achievement but affronted his old college in which he had served as a professor, as well as its president to whom he owed his academic career. The reactions of both men were natural but most unfortunate.

My Aunt Mary, the second daughter, married Dr. Henry P. Quincy and lived in nearby Dedham, which left Uncle Brooks alone of the family to take over the Old House at his mother's death in 1889. My grandmother had outlived her husband by several years and during that lonely time, when she was an invalid, Uncle Brooks looked after her conscientiously, though he could hardly have qualified as a cheerful companion. I shall, in a later chapter, write more fully about Uncle Brooks and his peculiarities and curious idiosyncrasies, for I knew him intimately for many years and was fond of him. It is enough to say here that shortly after his mother's death he married Miss Evelyn Davis and took over the Old House as his permanent home.

These were the personalities that were associated with the Old House when I first became aware of its significance. As I look back upon the Uncles, I see them as always writing — Uncle Charles in a nice square house just below his own on President's Hill, which he had bought to provide space for his books and to insure him peace from the distractions of a growing family, and which he called the "Annex." Uncle Henry when he was in Quincy commanded undisputed possession of the Stone Library, while Uncle Brooks reigned in John Adams's study on the second floor of the Old House. It used to puzzle me what they all found to write about, for my father never seemed to write at all — but when I asked him about it, he said, "I suppose it amuses them!" When I asked why he too did not write, he said that he had done all his writing when he was young and had nothing more to say now.

I knew the Old House as a wonderful playground. The garden, ruled by the gentle hand of Patterson the gardener, was always a mass of bloom in season and the carefully tended paths were simply an invitation for racing. Inside the house the attics were a mine of treasures. There in the cramped rooms on the third floor behind the dormer windows, which according to my father were hellish in summer and colder than Greenland in winter, lurked old trunks in which to rummage, full of discarded dresses and old-fashioned furbelows — an endless source of useless and forgotten odds and ends of former fashions. Downstairs in the Long Parlor among Abigail's French furniture were albums crowded with photographs of past dignitaries, foreign and domestic, and again books and odd bibelots everywhere. Quite unconsciously our generation felt about the Old House just as we did about the library, and rummaged there at will, but with a certain instinctive respect.

But the house did not come into true focus for me until the fateful summer of 1893, when, as a result of the financial panic then sweeping the country, our family was supposed to be on the brink of bankruptcy. All of the Adams brothers with the exception of the careful and uninterested Henry were badly extended financially and seriously involved, for they were a borrowing lot without much business sense. Brooks, who was a nervous creature with little self-control, was so apprehensive that he sent a hurry-up call to Henry in Europe to come home at once and give the family the benefit of his advice — and probably of his credit too. He came; relieved Uncle Brooks's mind by endorsing his paper, and then stayed on for the rest of the summer in Quincy to bolster up Brooks's nerves. When they managed to get off the subject of the panic, Uncle Henry discussed the theories of social revolution with Brooks, who was then struggling with his latest book, sub-

sequently called *The Law of Civilization and Decay.*
Brooks admired his brother so much that he could not re-
sist the opportunity, handed him by the panic, of picking
Henry's brains at his leisure. For some weeks Henry bore
it bravely, for he was fond of Brooks and interested in his
ideas, but as the days went on he found himself nervously
exhausted by Brooks's persistence. Finally he could stand
no more of Brooks's continual pressure, and when things
began to look more cheerful and it seemed almost likely
that we would not become paupers, he escaped to the peace
of the World's Fair at Chicago and the delights of discov-
ering the Dynamo.

As for me, I did not quite know what it was all about, but
I smelled tragedy as I saw my father wilt under the strain
and began to realize that something had hit him very hard.
Not so Uncle Charles, who, with more resilience, said that
he had never lost a night's sleep over the panic. My father
was by no means so nervously stable, and he never recovered. I had a sudden vision of a world that was not all
a bed of roses, but when autumn came and the worst was
over, we, like the rest of the world, packed up our troubles
and made for Chicago too.

CHAPTER THREE

A WORD about my father — and it may be quite a long word — for I cannot dismiss him as just an unsuccessful politician, amateur farmer and indifferent businessman. The adjectives may describe his career but they do not in the least describe the man himself. He was a very unusual and delightful person with great natural abilities, enormous personal charm, a lovely sense of humor, and a completely vigorous, balanced, independent and coura-

25

geous mind. He was born in September 1833, the second child and first son of Charles Francis Adams, and was named for his grandfather, John Quincy Adams, the sixth President. He grew up in Quincy which he always considered his home although later the family moved to Boston for the winter months. His brother Charles, only a year his junior, spoke of him while they were in college as essentially a good fellow with a very charming and endearing personality and cordial manners, and his brother Henry described him as "one of the best talkers in Boston society and perhaps the most popular man in the State though apt to be on the unpopular side." Henry also wrote later to a friend who was coming to Boston: "I hope that you will meet my brother John — he is the best and ablest of the lot, the sort of fellow who could make you laugh when the ship was sinking." Uncle Brooks often told me how jealous he had always been of my father for possessing those social qualities of charm and conviviality which he himself so painfully lacked, adding in the same breath that John was far too lazy ever to make effective use of them.

As little boys my father and his brother Charles were sent to a small school in nearby Hingham, but subsequently he went to the Boston Latin School before entering Harvard where he graduated with the Class of '53. My father then studied law for two years and was admitted to the Suffolk Bar. Later he hung up his shingle in Quincy, and there is a notice in the Quincy *Patriot* of 1858 that "John Quincy Adams may be found at his office on Mondays and

Tuesdays — at such and such a time." That "may" is very indicative of the man and does not sound as if his practice was either large or active, or as if he was very energetic in pursuit of professional success. To bear this out, there is a story of Father in his mature years when he had acquired a reputation and was, presumably, a responsible lawyer. One of his more important clients, finding that his case was coming up in court very shortly, tried in vain to find Mr. Adams whom he had engaged to defend him. After a long chase, my father was finally discovered placidly fishing for smelts in one of the isolated salt creeks of the Quincy shore. When hailed with the summons he refused to leave his sport but volunteered to write a note to the judge satis- factorily explaining his absence. Judge Horace Gray, who was later to be an Associate Justice of the United States Supreme Court, was certainly a sport himself, for on read- ing the hastily scribbled note he merely instructed the clerk to continue Mr. Adams's case "as he had been detained on important business." The note, on later inspection, read: "Dear Judge, for the sake of old Isaac Walton please put my case over, — the smelts are biting and I can't leave." It was a disarmingly flippant excuse, but no one with a true reverence for the law would have taken such a liberty with his vocation.

In his early manhood, my father made his sacrifice to family loyalty, although I doubt if he ever considered it in that light. He became engaged in 1860 to Miss Fanny Crowninshield of Boston and was preparing to be married the following spring, but by then the Civil War had broken out and almost immediately President Lincoln appointed John's father, Charles Francis Adams, to be United States Minister to England. It was a vitally important post for which the elder Adams with his well-balanced and sagacious mind was particularly well fitted, but, contingent on his accepting the post was the question of which of his four sons could, or would, stay at home and attend to his private affairs. John was the obvious choice. Charles, the second son, was unmarried and was preparing to go into the army, Henry was to go with his father as private secretary, and Brooks, the youngest, was still a schoolboy. So it was settled. My father was married at once and went to live in the Old House in Quincy, and immediately afterwards his father sailed for his station in London, to be gone over seven years. During that difficult and trying time, my father stood behind him at home and tried to take the burden of private responsibilities off his shoulders. The correspondence between the two men is pathetically revealing. It pictures my father struggling on unfamiliar ground but writing cheerfully and trying to satisfy his father and carry out his instructions — and the older man considerate and affectionate, but so harassed by duties in a country whose government was, during the war years, distinctly hostile that he was not always able to appreciate that affairs at home were chaotic too and could not necessarily go as he wanted them to. In theory my father liked farming, but liking farming and wringing a profit

from the arid soil of Quincy were two very different prop-
ositions, and even while he contended with the droughts
and the idiosyncrasies of the salt hay crops, his thoughts
must often have been with his friends who were fighting
and dying on the southern battlefields. I think that the im-
print of those frustrating years never left him for all that
his private life was a very full and happy one. My father
was a staunch supporter of Lincoln throughout the war
and was locally an ardent Republican, serving one term in
the Massachusetts House as well as being a member of
Governor Andrew's staff, but during the impeachment
times, with their disordered party squabbles that followed
the assassination of Lincoln, he could not reconcile himself
to what he considered the mistaken reconstruction policies
of the radical Republicans, and bolted the party to become
a Liberal Democrat. A wiser man who was a more far-
sighted and practical politician would have realized the fu-
tility of such precipitate action and would have seen how
much more effective it would be to work within the party
and not to further disrupt it when it was in such a state of
ferment, but, unfortunately, my father was an individualist
and not a politician — still less a practical one. He considered that President Johnson's stand on reconstruction was
essentially the same as Lincoln's had been, and that it was
the safest and speediest program, involving the least tam-
pering with the Constitution. But there was no holding the
Republican hotheads who had the bit in their teeth and
were preaching the extremes of retaliation and confiscation

as punishment to the conquered South, and that policy he could not stomach.

That the party was split wide open did not particularly interest my father who did not value party solidarity at such a price, and could not at any time tolerate political dictation. He was a lone wolf who had tasted blood. His gesture of resigning, however ill-advised, was very characteristic of his independent spirit, nor would he have hesitated if he had been able to foresee that in so doing he lost any chance of political preferment, for the Democratic party did not come into power again until the election of Grover Cleveland in 1884, by which time my father had lost his youthful zest and energy and could not bring himself to accept either the foreign mission or the seat in the Cabinet as Secretary of the Navy that Cleveland offered him. He had become too set in his ways to face the responsibility of a new and untried position for which he felt totally unprepared. It was indolence too, I imagine, and a desire to be left alone, though in all honesty to my father it must be said that political preferment was the last thing that he ever wanted; as he tersely put it in writing to his father in London: "I am fond of a shindy and I like a minority."

And it was this feeling of exhilaration and pleasure in a fight that drew him, in his youth, into his short career as the Young Lion of the Bay State Democracy. With his party's enthusiastic backing he had a wonderful time. He was five times a candidate for the Governorship between

1867 and 1871, and he also represented his native Quincy in four Legislatures, being in some mysterious way elected to the House twice, while being at the same time defeated for the Governorship. His party was in a hopeless minority and he could not possibly have anticipated political success, nor do I believe that he really wanted it, but he did want to live up to his own conception of a fighting minority as the keystone to a sound democracy. He spoke extremely well, not only with wit and vigor but with honest conviction, and although nothing can be duller than outdated political speeches, the few of his that still survive can to this day be read with interest. He was never a bore. His leadership was marked by outstanding frankness, courageous candor and a complete disregard of any party domination. Although he worked his hardest for his party and its success, he had to be allowed to do it without restraint or hindrance — and for himself he always accepted defeat with an entirely good-natured philosophy. He seems positively to have reveled in lost causes, if we can judge by his rather heated reply to his father, who, in the kindness of his heart, had written him a letter of sympathy in his defeat, while also suggesting, in the most tactful way, that there might be future compensations.

> As to the trouble, pain, and expense of my politics, [my father wrote] I hope that you do not think that I did it for a reward. I do trust that you know me to be sincere when I say that I do not wish, and would shun, any political honors. Once and for all understand me — do —

when I assure you on my honor, that absurd as it may look, I took my line last fall solely from a sense of duty and because I felt that the time demanded that an insignificant person like myself do his little d——est. I see now that you consider my views Quixotic — but I neither expected or hoped for success nor desired notoriety or applause — if it had been a winning cause I would not have touched it.

It is hard to deal justly with a man like that — a man who though well qualified for high office prefers the fight to the victory — which moves me to continue further with that blistering letter that he wrote to his amiable father who, after all, was only trying to sympathize with him.

Now, Sir, it is not that I am disappointed, it is just this in politics which I see even in you that jars me, you can't see that a man is honest all the way through and has no ambition. Even you think of your own son that embracing a lost cause from a pure sense of right was a folly if he did not expect some compensation in the long run. And Henry — a philosopher, takes for granted that I should have modified my course if I had forseen the President's. How humiliating it is that with my name I should wait for such trifles as that. [I am glad to say that at the end of the letter his native humor revived a little, for he finishes on a lighter touch.] And now Sir I hope that I have sufficiently exposed your humiliating position and glorified my own immaculate purity, bright aspirations and lovely character and if I have succeeded in doing so my toil has not been altogether in vain.

Although my father's political activities were purely local and never became a matter of national importance, his
views on current questions did attract wide attention and
in 1868, the presidential year when Grant was heading the
Republican ticket against the Democratic Seymour and
feeling was running high, he was asked by General Wade
Hampton and the Democratic Committee of South Carolina to come there and speak on the vexed problems of
reconstruction policies while at the same time giving himself the opportunity to study at first hand the attitude of
the southern people toward these difficult and vital questions. He hesitated at first to go, saying bluntly in his reply that he might say some very unwelcome things. He
was frank in stating that he felt that the North's distrust of
the South was largely based upon the unwise legislation
passed by the southern states in what were known as the
"black codes" and "vagrant laws" — and did not think
that under the circumstances it was wise for him to accept
the invitation, believing that as a tableau his appearance
would be a failure. The Committee, however, prevailed
on him to reconsider and he made several speeches in
South Carolina, notably in Charleston and Columbia. He
introduced himself as "the grandson of the earliest oppo-
nents of your peculiar institutions, an ardent supporter of
Lincoln in the active prosecution of the war, and as one
who hailed with gratitude the abolition of slavery." After
a terse recital of the fundamental principles underlying the
war he went into a careful and detailed discussion of the

reconstruction legislation, and urged most strenuously the cheerful acceptance of the results of the war. He spoke of the relations between the blacks and the whites, and to both gave friendly advice, while he challenged the audience to tell him if any one of them would restore slavery if it were possible; if any of them would restrain free speech; or if any of them would, in any contingency, contemplate the renewal of the rebellion even in the event of Grant's election or of continued coercive legislation. He ended on a high note of hope when he summoned up the memory of the old associations between South Carolina and Massachusetts and invoked the obligations that common interests imposed. The newspaper reports gave his conclusions as follows and I think that they are worth quoting, for he was handling dynamite when he thus addressed an audience in such a place at such a time.

Let us forgive and forget. With slavery its cause let our feelings cease. Let good will and brotherly love cast out all bitterness and let us all hasten the day when South Carolina and Massachusetts may stand once more, hand in hand under the old roof tree and under the old flag. I have carefully avoided any attempt to stir your feelings or amuse your minds. It did not seem to me an occasion for eloquence, if I had it, or humor, if I felt it. I am deeply and seriously impressed with the difficulties under which you labor and the dangers which threaten our system of government, and I have spoken seriously because I felt serious. Whatever may come of it I shall feel amply rewarded if, by any chance, I may have turned one heart to a calm, earnest, patient, honest effort to forward, as far as in it lies, the restoration of the · Constitution and the Union.

His feeling of the necessity for conciliation is vaguely reminiscent of his great-grandfather John Adams's address to King George the Third of England when he was presented to him as the first minister to his court from the new United States: "I hope that I may be instrumental in restoring the old good nature and good humor between people, who, though separated by an ocean and under different governments, have the same language, a similar religion and kindred blood." Knowing my father, I feel sure that he was not consciously imitating his great-grandfather, for though he respected his forebears, he was not given to any form of ancestor worship. In fact, it was only in naming me that he showed any weakness in that direction, but for that he certainly never apologized — only insisting that "Abigail was the best of the lot." I don't suppose that my father pleased anyone by his remarks in South Carolina, any more than John Adams could have pleased King George — peacemakers are seldom sympathetic to belligerents — but I don't really imagine that he expected to. Feelings still were taut and violent and neither side was ready for a calm unbiased view of the situation. Still, on the whole, the criticisms were respectful and he was honored for his effort to calm a little the passionate feelings of reconstruction politics.

My father was torn between his desire for a quiet life and his innate feeling of public obligation. His natural indolence and his interest in public affairs were continually at war, and even when he was most relaxed and peaceful, twinges of conscience would trouble him which he would try to relieve with what he called his "little amusements" — writing articles for friendly newspapers or organizing correspondence with men whose acquaintance he had made through his speeches. As he put it, rather naively, "The thought and study exercise my mind and make me comfortable."

Although his lack of ambition was probably tainted with laziness, he never shirked his responsibilities to his fellow townsmen. Year after year he presided as Moderator at the Quincy town meetings, until from rowdy gatherings of several days' duration, they became, under his firm management, business assemblies run with order and precision. The Quincy School Committee under his Chairmanship, backed by the enthusiastic energy of his brother Charles, developed a system of public administration that became a model for the entire state. He never spared himself in giving his best to his community in years of disinterested, faithful and devoted public service. When asked each year if he would run again for Moderator, he always replied, "Yes, if you will help me." If he was at times considered bluff, he was in truth robust with none of the weaknesses of rudeness and irritability, and he did his best in his own sphere to be a strong and useful public servant. Beyond his own town he did his part in the larger community. He served as a member of the Rapid Transit Commission appointed by Governor Russell and wrote a voluminous report on its findings, but I am afraid that that particular problem was as insoluble then as it is today. From 1877 till his death he was a member of the Harvard Corporation, which was perhaps as much an honor as a public service.

Under a brusque exterior he did his best to hide a warm heart, but at times even his abrupt manner could not entirely conceal it. A distressed barber who had rented a shop from my father for many years called on him to pay some money on his back rent which was badly in arrears. Much disturbed he stated his case. "Well," said Mr. Adams, "what are you kicking about? Don't you kick till I do." Later when the new Adams block was built in Quincy my father showed his friend the barber up to a nice front room and said, "How will this suit you?" That was typical of him and just as typical was his habit of sending bills receipted in advance to his tenants each month — for as I have said, he was an indifferent businessman.

Why have I written so much about a man who never held high office and who cannot in the nature of things have any claim to public remembrance? Perhaps because I like to think of him as a fine example of the best that we produce here in this country. He had wit, education, a knowledge of the law, a gift of oratory, popular manners and great social charm, and though he never attained his full stature, he was still a distinguished and public-spirited citizen. I was young when he died, but I have a curiously vivid memory of him and of his disarming way of treating me as a mature and responsible human being, and accepting my interests at my own valuation. I fished with him and he built wigwams with me in the woods. He sailed with me in my boat, and though he gave me first-rate instruction, I did the sailing and when I got her into irons it was my blunder, and I learned my lesson and did not let it happen a second time. It was the same with riding. When he thought that I could look after myself he let me ride any horse on the place, expecting me to use my own judgment, recognize my mistakes and accept responsibility for them. It was all on a mature level and made for a most satisfactory companionship with none of that superiority complex on his part, or inferiority on mine, that so often poisons the relationship between parent and child. He had a lot to teach me, but of course I did not have the sense to realize that — and perhaps it was just as well, for if I had shown any tendencies toward sitting at his feet or regarding him as an oracle, he would have undoubtedly thought me a horrid little prig. For all his devotion to me, he never would have tolerated any exhibition of fatuous sentimentality. My father never preached and he seldom advised, but he silently set before me — to take or to leave as I saw fit — the highest standards of decent behavior.

CHAPTER FOUR

WITH THE ADVENT of '94 it became increasingly
evident that my father was still in poor shape and it
was decided that a change of scene might be helpful, so in
January off we started, my parents, my oldest brother
George and myself. The southern route to the Mediter-
ranean ports was then becoming fashionable, and we sailed
on one of the new German luxury liners at that time being
turned out for the tourist trade. Our ship had been built

rather with a view to supplying luxuries than to withstanding the crudities of the North Atlantic in winter, and before we could reach gentler waters she ran into a winter gale. She shipped a couple of heavy seas one morning (they were reported as "tidal waves" in the Press), which stove in her flimsy superstructure and flooded her main decks. My mother and I were terrified when water poured into our stateroom and we heard the compartment doors being closed, but at least it instantly cured us of our seasickness, while the excitement did my father a world of good. He had always been nautically minded, but as he had never been across the ocean before, a storm at sea was a new experience and he reveled in it. My mother and I were naturally annoyed. After being smashed up, our ship rather pusillanimously turned tail and went back to New York for repairs, wallowing around and laying over on her beam-ends in the most alarming way as she did so. When we arrived, feeling flat and deflated, Uncle Charles miraculously appeared, announcing that he was sailing for Europe the next day and that we must go with him.

This time we arrived safely in England and from there moved slowly down to Italy where we passed a quiet winter, returning to Quincy by midsummer. The trip had failed to help my father and shortly after his return he had a severe stroke, from which he never rallied, and by August he was dead. With his death new responsibilities fell on my shoulders. Being the only daughter, I had not only to stay at home with my mother but also to help her cope with some of her new problems, none of which I had ever tackled before, so that it was not until the following spring that I began to feel my oats again, and it was then that Uncle Henry first stepped into the breach.

One of my close friends at Miss Folson's school on Chestnut Street in Boston was Molly Hooper, youngest daughter of Mr. Edward Hooper who was Uncle Henry's brother-in-law. Mr. Hooper was a widower with five daughters, and I liked nothing so much as to pass a night at his house on Fayerweather Street in Cambridge. The house was in reality two separate houses joined together by a covered passageway. That was in itself exciting and unique, and the five girls made the house exceptional. Mr. Hooper was the quietest of men, but no one could have been kinder. He was a connoisseur and authority on art who deeply impressed everyone with his taste and judgment. His house was entirely simple and unpretentious but was full of exquisite things — Blake drawings and fine Winslow Homers and La Farge watercolors. My visits to the Hoopers were a revelation to me. It was Mr. Hooper who suggested one evening that I should go down with Molly and his eldest daughter Ellen to Uncle Henry's in Washington for the coming spring vacation. The only hitch was that I must invite myself, as one of Uncle Henry's little idiosyncrasies was that he would ask no one to his house. Mr. Hooper felt, very properly, that being a niece I could propose myself. Rather fearfully I did so and received the following letter by return mail.

22 April [1895]

Dear Hitty

I am enormously pleased that one of my own nieces should at last think it worth while to make me a visit. Come along and stay a month! Never mind waiting for the Hoopers! I am pretty stupid and the place is pretty dull, but I guess we can have a good time.

Affely ys
HENRY ADAMS

Poor man, he little realized what he was letting himself in for and that from that time up to his death, twenty-three years later, I should be continually popping in and out of his house.

That first trip was wonderful. The journey was an all-day one with a pleasant interlude in the middle when the train was bodily shunted onto a ferryboat and taken around New York to the Jersey City terminal. Uncle Henry met us at the dreary old station in Washington. I had not seen him for several years and he couldn't but suggest the White Rabbit in *Alice in Wonderland* with his small hands and little kid gloves. His house on H Street — long since demolished to make room for the Hay-Adams Hotel — was a dream of comfort and charm, a charm that familiarity never lessened. It was designed by his friend and classmate Henry H. Richardson, and was a fine example of the use of the Romanesque arch adapted to domestic architecture. One entered a low hall while above were the living rooms — a big one in the front looking out on Lafayette Square with its prancing equestrian statue of a most complacent Andrew Jackson. Also on the front of the house was Uncle Henry's study. In the rear was the dining room which overlooked a pleasant tree-shaded yard enclosed by a stable at the back. Two admirable colored servants ran the house — William the butler and Maggie the maid. There were others concealed downstairs, including a cook who could make particularly hearty gumbo soup and plank a shad to the queen's taste.

Uncle Henry's study was furnished with a huge mahogany table which took up most of the room. At this desk he could be found every morning drinking his coffee and ponderously making notes in his exquisite script. He never scribbled his notes on scratch pads; they were inscribed as meticulously as if he were engraving them for posterity. Nor was he disturbed when the usual quota of the young and unoccupied of both sexes drifted in for a review of the most recent gossip. He loved to hear their comments on the latest social mistakes and current absurdities of the newer and more flamboyant hostesses — insisting that, as he was a complete recluse, his friends must take pity on him and keep him up-to-date. He always gave these morning visitors a cordial welcome with never a hint that they might be interrupting his work — or that his work was of any consequence — for he evidently enjoyed the talk and chatter and did not mean to discourage it even by the simple expedient of shutting his door. On the contrary he always welcomed us with a cheery "Hullo, infants, how are

you this morning?" and when we replied in kind he invariably answered, "Wuss — considerably wuss." This was the
standard ritual.

The living room opened out of his study and was larger
and more formal. It combined distinction with masculine
comfort, while being at the same time very characteristic
of his individual taste. It held two low curved sofas and
some equally low leather armchairs, all chosen for his con-
venience, while a few chairs of more standard size catered
to the comfort of his taller friends. One chair in particular
— which we regarded as a species of throne — was always
brought forward and placed in a commanding position
when his friend Mrs. John Hay came to dinner, for she was
a large woman and could not easily lower herself onto one
of his more oriental couches. Other women may have been
accorded this courtesy, but with Mrs. Hay it was routine.
Uncle Henry himself used this seat when he played his

nightly game of solitaire. There were shoulder-high book-
cases around his living room hung with pieces of Chinese
brocade, and above were some of his collection of pictures
which were scattered everywhere all over the house.
There were many examples of English eighteenth and
nineteenth century watercolors — De Wints, Cotmans,
Coxes and Girtins — while the dining room held two notable Turner oils — an early one of Norwich cathedral over
the fireplace and on the opposite wall a later one of a characteristically luminous whaling ship. In his study were
many drawings including a weird and repulsive Blake oil of
Nebuchadnezzar on all fours eating grass, a picture that
had a grisly fascination for me.

At the time of that first visit I took everything complacently in my stride, but I realize now what a fearful
bore it must have been for Uncle Henry to have two
gawky and unsophisticated girls dumped upon him, especially as he really put himself out a good deal for us,
though in theory we were supposed to look after ourselves
and not be a nuisance. Shortly after our arrival, perhaps to
start us off properly, he took us on a sightseeing tour.
How he must have hated it, self-conscious New Englander
that he was, as we trailed after him exclaiming at everything that we saw. We began with the Capitol and I love
to remember Uncle Henry's delighted expression of horror
as he pointed out the mammoth picture of the Battle of
Lake Erie which hangs on one of the monumental marble
stairways, and said, "There, infants, is a fine example of our

great American Art." I had been prepared to admire it until I saw his face and had a faint glimmering of what discrimination might mean. He groaned happily over the statues in the Rotunda, but was at some pains to find the tablet in the floor which marks the place where his grandfather John Quincy Adams fell — stricken by paralysis at his seat in Congress.

From the Capitol we went to the State Department, which I characterized in my diary as a "bore," and then finished up with the White House on our way home.

Molly and I were too young to enter into any of the Washington social life, but in Uncle Henry's house it was hard to avoid touches of it, for it came to you unsolicited. He had made it a rule that he would never accept any social invitation, but his friends ignored this eccentricity and came to his house instead, and no day passed but that one or more, and often five or six of his intimates, would drop in for either breakfast or dinner. Breakfast was the French *déjeuner à la fourchette* which was served at noon. It was all quite simple and places were put on or taken off as occasion demanded, and by some miracle of good luck, or good management on William's part, I have no recollection of the food ever running short. The one exception to Uncle Henry's inflexible rule was his daily tea with Mr. and Mrs. John Hay. He always had an afternoon walk with Mr. Hay followed by tea at the Hay house next door. Hay had been a close friend since the early days of the Lincoln administration when he had come to Washington as secretary to the new President and met Adams who was serving his father, a member of Congress, in the same capacity. Later the friendship had been renewed when the Hays made Washington their permanent home and the two had ended by building houses side by side on Lafayette Square.

Uncle Henry's intimates not only dropped in for breakfast or dinner whenever they wanted to, but they also felt free to bring any guest who they thought would be an addition to the circle. Usually that worked well, but occasionally someone would be introduced who could not be treated in quite such a cavalier fashion. There was a Spanish ambassador, for example, who, having been brought to the house by some mutual friend, felt at liberty afterwards to call up and invite himself. When he did so, Uncle Henry would get hold of some charming woman to come and do the honors for him. No one could have been a more delightful host than Uncle Henry — gay and amusing with a wonderful faculty for keeping the ball rolling and stimulating light conversation — and so long as no one was argumentative or controversial, everything was perfect. He contended that the dinner table was no place for dispute or altercation, and his rule that serious things must be discussed lightly and light things seriously made on the whole a pretty satisfactory formula for dinner-party conversation. You might touch on foreign affairs flippantly but you must discuss the latest gossip in all seriousness. Occasionally the situation would get out of hand when some contrary spirit like Uncle Brooks or Senator Lodge would get restless and exasperated under this system and, feeling that the pleasant inanity had gone far enough, would start to argue or pontificate on some burning issue of the moment. That would destroy Uncle Henry's light touch. But usually the guests were amenable, particularly the women, and delighted to play Uncle Henry's game, so that the talk always remained serene.

Every now and then, however — and I look back on those occasions with horror — a characteristically Adams gloom would descend on Uncle Henry. Glooms were common to all the brothers and even my more normal father was not entirely immune. Uncle Charles could retire into depths of complete detachment, while Uncle Brooks's low spirits were simply appalling. Perhaps these depressions were due to boredom, to which affliction all the brothers were unduly sensitive, but for an onlooker these moods were an agonizing experience, during which one was left impotently trying to cope with the expiring conversation. Luckily this seldom happened with Uncle Henry, for he was naturally sociable and enjoyed women's society. He was always at pains to draw ladies out, insisting that they were all more intelligent and better informed than their husbands.

It always astonished me that Uncle Henry's critics should make such a circumstance of his amiable little foibles and pretenses. Certainly he had many facets; that was part of his charm, and it had amused him to build up a social myth about himself. He knew that he was a picturesque figure and he did not want to be taken too seriously in any of his phases. It delighted him to speak of himself as a Cardinal and he loved to refer to his "Hat," or else, more cynically, described himself as only a stable companion for statesmen. His pose as a recluse was perhaps justified, for he did not mingle in the world outside of his own house, but in reality this was a blind for living exactly as he wanted to — he did not want to go out in society; dinners bored him and he much preferred that his friends should bring the pick of the world to his house where he could enjoy them without any social responsibility. He was considered by his adoring nieces as the source of all wisdom and we would sit at his feet drinking in every word. We forced the role of guide, philosopher and friend upon him, but he played up to it delightfully, for he liked young people and our starry-eyed veneration must have pleased him. He would listen to us with great patience, but he never took our problems too seriously and would banter us along, being very careful not to give us any direct suggestions or advice. I am sure that he did not want to run any risk of our saying, "Uncle Henry said so and so." In fact his rule about any form of repetition was drastic and unequivocal: "You ought to be shot for quoting what anyone says — you never get it straight and it may do endless harm." And then he would add, "Have your own ideas but keep off other people's." He certainly was kind and wise with a lovely sense of humor and had great patience with our fawning affection. His brother Brooks, however, could not see anything funny in the idea of Uncle Henry as a Cardinal, nor was he amused when Uncle Henry referred to himself as a "Conservative Christian Anarchist"; for Brooks these flights of fancy were too trivial for a sensible man. Brooks did not like whimsey and when he came down to Washington to talk to his brother he meant to talk sensibly or know the reason why. It never occurred to him that Uncle Henry was trying to escape from just that. They were curiously different, the two brothers, although they liked and admired each other. Brooks was primarily a man of action. When public questions arose he wanted to put his oar in and say what he thought, unmindful of the fact that no one was going to listen to him. It took years of bitter disappointment to get that through his head.

However, that spring when I first visited him, all of Uncle Henry's social formulas went by the board when Theodore Roosevelt (just leaving for New York to become Police Commissioner) burst in to breakfast with John Hay, Mr. Rockhill and Mr. Phillips. Mr. Rockhill was a distinguished Orientalist and Mr. Phillips a well-loved Washington lawyer, who was devoted to Uncle Henry and took his nieces under special protection. That breakfast was a revelation of the power of energy, enthusiasm and charm. With Uncle Henry to egg him on, Roosevelt not only led the conversation but dominated it, and his talk was so spontaneous and his charm so infectious that I wanted him to keep it up indefinitely. I am not so sure that the men felt entirely that way, but Mr. Roosevelt's dynamic

personality, combined with his humor and his abounding
energy, made a profound impression on me, which subse-
quent meetings never modified.

One pleasant spring day we made an excursion down the
Potomac to Chapawomsik, a small island off Quantico,
Virginia, where a group of Washingtonians ran a mild
shooting and fishing club. Our party consisted of Chandler
Hale, a young scion of the Hale dynasty of Maine, with
Tom Lee, a gentle sporting character from Boston who
preferred the simple life to the hazards of State Street and
Boston banking. In the club at the same time was Professor
Langley, a delightfully enthusiastic scientist who was ex-
perimenting with a crude machine in which he hoped to fly.
The machine sat in the river looking thoroughly waterlogged, and I doubt if it ever moved from there. As for
the rest of us, we fished under Tom Lee's tutelage and
then ate enormous quantities of planked shad. We came
back by train the next day, but stopped on our way at
Mount Vernon, as the conscientious Uncle had said, "The
infants must not miss the best thing in America." That
ended our first visit.

The next Easter Mr. Hooper took his daughters, Fanny
and Molly, and me down to Uncle Henry's. By this time
we felt like sophisticated women of the world and plunged

at once into the excitement of the stirring political cam-
paign for Cuba Libre which, in the spring of 1896, was
convulsing Washington. A revolt against the corrupt administration of Spain had broken out in Cuba the previous
year, and was being put down with ferocious cruelty by
the Spanish General Weyler. By the spring of '96, egged
on and inflamed by the Hearst and Pulitzer presses in New
York, anti-Spanish feeling had risen to fever heat in the
United States and pressure was being brought to bear on
President Cleveland to recognize the insurgents. Senators
Lodge of Massachusetts and Cameron of Pennsylvania were
the leaders in the Senate of the Cuba Libre movement, and
long and bitter debates were going on in both houses over
a resolution for recognition proposed by Senator Cameron.
Uncle Henry's house was a hotbed of Cuban enthusiasm, for
not only were both Senators — Lodge and Cameron — of
his intimate circle, but the cause itself appealed strongly to
his sporting instincts. Still he was in something of a delicate
position, as the able head of the Cuban Junta in New York,
a fiery little gentleman called Gonzalo de Quesada, had been
brought to his house and had found its atmosphere so congenial and useful that he continued to frequent it. That
was all very well, but the Spanish Ambassador, Dupuy de
Lome, had also been a guest at Uncle Henry's table and
might, quite possibly, pop in again at any moment, so that
Señor Quesada had to be very circumspect in his visits.
Of course we girls were thrilled at the Cuban patriot who
was not only handsome, but who appealed to us as a sort of

modern George Washington — not only a rebel and a patriot in the best Washington tradition, but complete with blue blood and vast estates. We haunted the galleries of the House and Senate to hear the debates on the Cameron resolution and were jubilant when it passed both Houses. I believe that it was never activated, as Secretary of State Olney maintained that recognition of a belligerent was the function of the Executive branch of the Government, and neither the President nor he felt that recognition was the wise policy at that time. Mr. Quesada was most polite and politic in his courtesy to us girls, calling us to Uncle Henry "his beautiful guests," which warmed our hearts. He also sent us gifts of Cuba Libre stamps as well as a small enameled pin of the Cuban flag which we had to raffle between us and which went to Molly.

Our visit was made socially supreme through the kindness of the Secretary of State, Richard Olney, and his daughter Mrs. Minot. The Secretary had been a friend of my father's, and when he heard through Mr. Hooper that I was down in Washington with his daughters he sent us all passes to the Diplomatic Gallery of the Senate so that we could haunt it to our heart's content. He followed that up by stopping at the house one morning to ask us if we would like to go across the way with him and see the President in the White House. We flew for our hats in ecstasies. It was all delightfully informal. President Cleveland was sitting at a big desk in a room at the head of the main staircase to which we were ushered up by the doorkeeper with no more ceremony than a nod from Mr. Olney. We were introduced to the President and he couldn't have been nicer — quite as if he were accustomed to having ardent young females descend upon him in the morning. He was very kind and appreciative about my father and gave us all roses from a big bunch on his desk. He was a heavily built man with a powerful head and shoulders, but he had a charming, rather shy smile and we all were perfectly delighted with his cordial reception, and enormously grateful to Mr. Olney for his kindness in giving us that pleasure. When later I recounted my adventures to Uncle Henry, he laughed and told of his being taken by his father to see President Taylor (which he wrote of in his *Education*) and of how the President's horse "Old Whitey" had been grazing on the lawn outside while the President inside was receiving callers as simply as if he had been in the paddock too. My brother Charlie also gave me his version of presidential calls when he described being taken by Uncle Henry himself to call upon President Harrison and how, while they waited for the President, Mrs. Harrison had regaled them with a detailed account of how she doctored her husband's sore throats with mustard plasters and a stocking. My experience was the best.

Our next excitement was when Mr. Olney asked us to dinner. It was my first real dinner party and I was tremendously excited. I sat on Mr. Olney's right and had a most wonderful time, feeling that at last I was in a fair way to becoming a woman of the world. Mrs. Minot, the Secretary's daughter, took us a few days later to a reception at the White House where we met Mrs. Cleveland as well as the President.

Molly, Fanny and I returned to Boston with our egos rather inflated, but we were soon put in our places, for Boston, as we knew it, was not interested in Cuba Libre — not at least until two years later when the *Maine* was blown up in Havana harbor, but by that time I was in Paris under the fiery guidance of Uncle Brooks.

CHAPTER FIVE

ALTHOUGH I HAVE already spoken of my Uncle Brooks Adams, I cannot embark on my long and intimate association with him without going a little farther into an account of his many conflicting traits and peculiarities. He started life under the handicap of being the youngest of a turbulent family of brothers and sisters — three brothers and two sisters, most of them strongly individualistic. He was one of those intelligent though irritating children who continually ask questions. His brother Henry once wrote of Brooks to his older brother Charles, "I think myself that we ought to try our hardest to tolerate the child, who is really a first rate little fellow, apart from his questions, and we ought not to snub him so much." That letter is characteristic of the two brothers, and where Brooks always irritated Charles, Henry rather affectionately put up with him with a toleration which later grew into genuine admiration and respect. Henry always found Brooks wearing, but he could listen to him patiently if he was reasonably explicit and then would say, "Perhaps you have got something there, Brooks." Of my father Brooks was deeply admiring, but mostly for his social qualities, which Brooks envied enormously, not possessing them himself. For Louisa, his oldest sister, Brooks had nothing but praise. She was not beautiful but in his estimation she had a more brilliant mind than Henry's.

Brooks, I feel sure, was well sat upon in his childhood and his disposition could not have been improved when, on his father's accepting the mission to England at the beginning of the Civil War, he was at once placed in a British boarding school, where his life was made utterly miserable by the open hostility of his schoolmates. Feeling among the upper classes in England was then red hot against the North, and the son of the American Minister had a poor time of it. He was not only ostracized but jeered at as "a rebel and a traitor." His family were too anxious and harassed over their own problems to bother much about the difficulties of a child of twelve, so Brooks got on as best he could. He always maintained that his familiarity with Scott and Marryat, both of whom he loved, and even with Dickens, whom he disliked, stemmed from his lonely years at that British school where the prejudice of the boys so completely isolated him that from lack of any social intercourse he fell back on reading. Later, when he came home to prepare for Harvard, he found that he had lost any faculty that he might have had for making friends. It was during those years and through part of his college course that he maintained a regular correspondence with his father in London. It was a curious affair. Brooks, like all boys, did not write often enough to suit his father, nor did he tell him in detail what he was doing, so that his father's letters are a continual admonition: "Your spelling is poor," and again, "You must be more careful of your grammar," allowing only a few lines for sympathy or interest, still less for any account of his own work in London.

Brooks, for all his admiration for his father, would occasionally rebel and his replies would become tense and irritable — but then he would write enthusiastically of his delight in Professor Gurney's lectures on Medieval History. The taste so started remained with him for life. To such letters his father would reply with such vague platitudes as "Education, deportment and character are the essential requisites to the enjoyment of what life has to give" — adding, "The foundation of these must be laid in youth if at all." In spite of these trite remarks, Brooks considered his father's standards so high that he could never hope to approach them himself, and it was this morbid admiration for his father that was the foundation of the sense of inferiority that made his own personality so complex and puzzling, for by instinct and nature he was a violent and savage man. Brooks was many-sided — brusque, intolerant, opinionated, cranky and tactless to the last degree — but in spite of these idiosyncrasies he was at bottom warm-hearted and infinitely loyal. His servants were all devoted to him, which was in itself a great tribute, for he was an exacting and demanding taskmaster. He was a complete medievalist. He approved of the subjugation of women and deplored any suggestion of their being granted the franchise. He always extolled the virtues of the martial man and the convent-bred woman. At bottom that explains his love for Scott's novels, which he always described as "bloody good reading." He really admired Scott's heroes because they typified courage and were not ruled by fear which he insisted was the motive behind Dickens's characters. Uncle Brooks was like a child in his love for the fighting man. I remember his writing to me, when I was shut up in a convent in Paris during the Spanish War, of a visit that he had paid to his nephew "Bay" Lodge on his ship, and of how well his new responsibilities as an officer became him. There was also an irritating letter that he wrote me at the time of the First World War when my husband was enrolled at the Officer's Training Camp at Plattsburg, New York. Uncle Brooks had gone up there to see for himself what the training amounted to and had received every possible attention from my husband who was sincerely fond of him. "My dear child," he wrote, "permit me to say that you don't half appreciate or know your husband. Bob appears at his best at Plattsburg, — many men do but he particularly well." He then went on to describe the camp and added, "The atmosphere is congenial to me, much more so than that of State Street." Uncle Brooks became very fond of my husband, which was a reward for Robert's efforts in that direction, for I used to ask him to spend five minutes every morning on the problem of liking Uncle Brooks — devoted as I was to my revered relation, I realized that he was an acquired taste.

Despite his general lack of social qualities, Uncle Brooks had several devoted friends dating from his college days — men like Cabot Lodge and Austin Wadsworth of the Genesee Valley clan — and he "made" the Porcellian Club while at Harvard. Brooks graduated from college with the Class of 1870. Like most of his family, he chose the law for his vocation, but not before he had told his friend Lodge that he would not go into any profession where he could not honestly say what he felt. It is said that Lodge's retort to that smug statement was completely realistic when he replied, "Well, that does not bother me." At any rate Brooks did graduate from the Harvard Law School and set up an office in Boston. Unfortunately his manners were calculated to discourage any prospective clients, for he felt himself quite at liberty to refuse any case where either the client or the proposed litigation failed to please him. Naturally his practice died on its feet. He could antagonize almost anyone at the drop of a hat. He recognized his limitations later in life, but he was powerless to cope with them and they discouraged and humiliated him to the end. He used to say, plaintively, "As soon as I join a group of people they all melt away and disappear," which was all only too true. His wife, trying for a light touch, used to say of him, "I call him Brook because Brooks is plural and he is singular." The poor man wrote a rather touching letter to his friend Cecil Spring-Rice, who for many years had been stationed in Washington in various positions in the British Embassy: "My dear fellow, I am a crank, very few people can endure to have me near them, but I like to be with you and I suppose that I like to be with those that are sympathetic — the more since there are very few." He wrote approximately the same thing to my husband, and I know that he always had it on his mind. "Henry," he would say, "can brighten his life with people, but people don't like me and have no patience with me; they won't even listen to what I have to say." It was all the worse as he was full of sentimentality and yearned for affection.

I never was quite sure of Uncle Brooks's sense of humor; some things amused him enormously, and yet his idea of a little light reading for a young woman recovering from an operation was Newman's *Apologia*. His marriage was in many ways as strange as his other goings on. After his mother's death, he decided that he must marry then if he was ever going to, and for that end he consulted his good friend Mrs. Cabot Lodge, who, very wisely and being very conscious of Brooks's really sterling qualities, suggested her own sister — Evelyn Davis. Brooks approved highly and at once took the young lady out buggy-riding. How soon they reached an agreement I do not know, but they were shortly engaged and were married not long afterwards. Uncle Brooks's love affairs were not always so well timed, for, as the story goes, he once proposed to a lady at a dinner party. When she refused him in no uncertain terms, he told her furiously that he had always known that she was a d——ed fool. At which, I believe, the lady fainted. At any rate the idea that anyone in their right mind would take on Brooks as a husband was received with some incredulity but great applause by the whole family, although perhaps my father expressed the general feeling when, on going to call on Miss Davis for the first time, he announced with a twinkle, "I am now going to pay my respects to the unfortunate lady who says that she is going to marry my brother Brooks." It was in that way that Uncle Charles and my father always referred to Brooks. He was either spoken of rather disparagingly as "my brother Brooks" or contemptuously as "that crank Brooks," all of which led me to think of him as some form of violent crackpot with unholy leanings to pessimism, sentiments which were, of course, anathema to his sturdy and optimistic older brothers. Miss Davis, who became Uncle Brooks's wife, was usually called "Daisy" by her friends, but Brooks at once vetoed that foolishness — he would not have her treated like a cow, he said; she must be Evelyn to all. She was a charming, gentle lady and we were all devoted to her.

Uncle Brooks had always been a rather nebulous figure to me until after his marriage in 1889, at which time he took over the Old House where he lived in the summers, renting a house in Boston for the winter months. He loved the Quincy place and took an enormous interest in renovating the house and restoring the garden, where he followed the original plan of John Adams. Living nearby in Quincy I saw both Aunt Evelyn and Uncle Brooks frequently, and as time went on I began to find Brooks increasingly sympathetic and understanding on that vital subject then nearest to my heart, horses and their training. I rode every day, and Brooks felt that as I had been taught by his old riding instructor and friend, Henri de Bussigny, I must have in me the makings of a decent horsewoman. De Bussigny was a Boston institution, much in the same category as Papanti the famous dancing master. He had been a cavalry officer in the French army, a product of St. Cyr, and was a good example of that rigid type. He was married to a characteristically efficient French wife who kept his accounts and looked after his pupils. It was at his dreary, dirty old riding academy on Albany Street that I had my first riding lessons, bumping solemnly around the ring, often with a stick in the small of my back between my elbows to insure that I sat up straight and did not slump. It was an impossible position for comfortable riding but it had style and distinction. De Bussigny was so well thought of that when the New Riding Club was organized by a group of enthusiasts in the early 1890's and a fine building put up on Hemenway Street at the edge of the Park, De Bussigny was installed there as riding master. A special little ring was added for his benefit where he could work in seclusion over his favorite *Haute École*. He was a first-rate horseman of the French classical school, but not a good teacher, as he would quickly become bored with the awkward efforts of a group of little girls. He would forget all about us for long periods of time, practicing the *Haute École*, and leaving us bouncing around the ring until we were utterly exhausted. Still on the whole he did well by us, for he did not let us get sloppy and certainly taught us that there was more to equitation than just staying on your pony. Our ponies had to do what we wanted or he must know the reason why. De Bussigny's training appealed to

Brooks's military mind and was the basis of his interest in me. He followed my activities all one summer, and by autumn we were fast friends, and his sarcastic manner had lost all its terrors for me.

One day he said to me, "My dear child, you are doing yourself no good in Quincy and as you are woefully ignorant you had better come over to Paris with your aunt and me this winter and learn a little French." No sooner said than done. My family were planning to spend that winter in Quincy and were only too glad to have me disposed of. Early in November, Uncle Brooks, Aunt Evelyn and I sailed from Boston on the S.S. *Canada* bound for Liverpool. Traveling with my uncle I soon discovered was quite an experience. He had to have a large supply of his favorite books taken with him, whether a library abroad would be available or not. They were his pets and he could not be parted from them, nuisances though they were.

Our first stop in England was at Harrogate, for Uncle Brooks must have his cure before the winter set in. Cures were his panaceas for all ills and a season without one was unthinkable. Harrogate is in Yorkshire, and Yorkshire in November is not at its gayest. With the short days and endless evenings Uncle Brooks literally wallowed in gloom. The sun set right after lunch and there was nothing whatever to do except watch Uncle Brooks drink the waters and then go for a little hygienic walk with him afterwards. Later, when we had survived the cure, we moved to London, stopping on the way at York and Lincoln for the ben-

efit of my education. London was hardly an improvement
on Harrogate, for we were installed in some cheerless
rooms in Clarges Street off Piccadilly. This was Brooks's
tribute to family sentiment, for the man who ran the establishment had been a respected retainer of his father's in
the sixties. Incidentally Brooks scorned hotels. Our food
was tasteless, the carpets threadbare, the beds cold and
lumpy, and the atmosphere outside was of the pea soup
variety.

How glad I was to leave London and reach Paris,
though even there my poor aunt was not allowed to rest,
as Brooks, resenting every night passed in a hotel, insisted
that we must set up housekeeping without a moment's delay. Luckily we shortly found a refuge in a miniature private house that suited him exactly. It was a darling mite of
a doll's house in the rue de Verneuil, a short street running off the rue des Saints Pères near the river on the left
bank. The house was complete with a tiny courtyard, resi-
dent concierge and an impressive gate with a grille. The
courtyard boasted a saucer-like basin, and the house itself
was as thin as a slice of bread. Inside, what rooms there
were all faced the courtyard and would have been flooded
with sun but for the voluminous red velvet hangings with
which the whole house both upstairs and downstairs was
smothered. These curtains were hung on huge wooden
rings, and when the *bonne à tout faire* went around pulling
them back in the morning they sounded like a volley of ar-
tillery and left no remnant of sleep behind them. The stair-

way was like the companionway of a ship, practically per-pendicular, with red velvet-covered ropes as a banister. There was no bathtub in this establishment, but tin tubs as minute as the rest of the house were concealed under the beds, while the beds themselves boasted mountains of feath-ers. It was a dream of a place.

We lived in the rue de Verneuil for three lovely months. Uncle Henry Adams we had found comfortably installed in an apartment near the Bois, where we saw a great deal of him since his aggressive brother Brooks, safely surrounded by females, seemed less overpowering than usual. Henry was very fond of Aunt Evelyn and he always enjoyed be-ing tutor to the young. At Christmas he showered Aunt Evelyn and myself with presents and was so pleased with the idea that I liked marrons glacées for breakfast that I was never without them. "Infant," he would say, "is there anything short of a camel that can touch the digestion of a growing girl?"

Brooks lost no time in making it clear to all concerned that there were more serious questions than candy, and he at once plunged into the job of translating his *Law of Civilization and Decay* into French — but not before he had produced a governess for me and started me off on my proper occupations. Mlle. Moynier was a typical intellec-tual, well-educated French woman, very plain and very nice. We roamed all over Paris together after I had done my regular stint of irregular verbs and *dictée*. She was de-lightfully active-minded and was just Uncle Brooks's cup

of tea. Uncle Brooks always insisted like Alice-in-Won-
derland that we should "never go anywhere without a
porpoise," and we never did. Usually our jaunts were to
some historical spot. In the afternoon when Uncle Brooks
relaxed from his labors, he would take me in hand, and our
goal was apt to be the Louvre or some other picture gallery — for he loved pictures and made me love them too,
though I was never allowed to linger in the galleries more
than half an hour at a time, on the safe principle that my
mind could not concentrate for longer than that. I never
knew whether Uncle Brooks's interest in pictures was
purely artistic or whether the subject matter interested him
more than the technique. His sightseeing was peculiar and
never varied. He would race into a gallery, looking neither
to the right or left until he had found what he wanted,
then he would plant himself before it and, oblivious of the
crowd which gathered around, would begin declaiming
whatever poetry he thought appropriate. For example, one
of his pets was Delacroix's "Sack of Constantinople" — a
thing of splendid color — and there he would start on
Macaulay's "Frothing white with many a plume, dark
blue with many a spear," until he would become conscious
of the growing curiosity around him and would move on
to Géricault's "Raft of the Medusa," where I would be
given a lecture on the gruesome tragedy depicted. Like
Uncle Henry, Brooks was a first-rate teacher, and I could
pass an examination on it now after all these years.

Uncle Brooks dearly loved to wallow in gloom, and a

disaster as a background for bravery always appealed to him — while human drama went to his head like wine. Hence, I suppose, his fondness for martial poetry in which he was like a little boy. I was taken regularly to the classical matinées at the Comédie Française, and though the verses might sound stilted and the sense melodramatic to my crude ears, the genius and diction of a Mounet-Sully or a Mme. Bartet lifted them to an extraordinary vitality. Now and then Uncle Brooks would try some modern production, but it was not often successful as, if anything off-color developed, I was unceremoniously dragged out. That was a dreadfully mortifying process. When, at probably the most exciting moment of the play, I would hear Uncle Brooks murmur to Aunt Evelyn, "My dear, this isn't quite the thing for Abigail," my heart would sink. Even Uncle Henry laughed at his brother's conventionality and would say, "My dear Brooks, even in Quincy little girls do grow up, you know," — but you couldn't change my revered relative as easily as that.

Uncle Henry was at that time awaiting the arrival in Paris of his friends Mr. and Mrs. John Hay, who were to join him on a trip to Egypt. Hay had been appointed by President McKinley Ambassador to the Court of St. James the previous April, and was now taking his allotted sixty days' leave of absence. When they arrived in January, Uncle Henry took us all, the Hays, the Brooks Adamses and myself to see one of the very early performances of Rostand's *Cyrano de Bergerac*, which, with Coquelin Cadet in the title role, was electrifying Paris. It was a marvelous evening — we had a box to ourselves and we all loved it, for even the sophisticated uncles were moved to enthusiasm — while I went completely off my head along with the rest of the audience.

On the duller side of life, I was occasionally taken to some typical French soirée of the intellectual variety — where we might be entertained by Uncle Brooks's publisher. There in a chilly salon we would sit in chairs arranged around the wall as though at some meeting. The women usually sat together on one side of the room and the men on the other; neither group seemed anxious for the other's society. The women made polite conversation while the men talked animatedly, although, as far as I could see, they had had no alcohol to spur them on. As a matter of fact, Uncle Brooks was apt to take it upon himself to do the spurring, for in his most courtly and labored French he would presently deliberately insult some savant, hoping in that way to "get him to talk," as he expressed it. Needless to say, his methods were never successful. In the meantime, Aunt Evelyn and I would cower among the ladies doing our best to atone for Uncle Brooks's rudeness but not knowing what to say or how to say nothing politely. The refreshments would be plates of little petit-fours and some kind of liquid in glasses which tasted vaguely of tisane, and then the evening would end with a nightmare of stilted good-byes.

During all this time Uncle Brooks was struggling over

his translation, while Aunt Evelyn and I tried ineffectively to help along by working at his index. Between the index and the problem of having Uncle Brooks's shirts ironed to his taste, Aunt Evelyn had a poor time, but Mlle. Moynier was a tower of strength and dealt with the washerwoman in a way that Aunt Evelyn was quite incapable of. As for myself, I went to all sorts of *cours* — diction and dancing especially — and on Sunday afternoons I would be taken to either the Lamoureux or Colonne Concerts in the hope that good music would cure my tone-deaf ears. We had a very happy time, and as Dr. William Sturgis Bigelow had arrived in Paris, he continued my supply of marron glacées when Uncle Henry departed for Egypt. Out of our quiet scholastic lethargy we were rudely awakened in February 1898 by the news of the sinking of the battleship *Maine* in Havana harbor.

CHAPTER SIX

T HE NEWS of the loss of the *Maine* with the implica-
tion that it had been blown up by Spanish treachery
was too much for Uncle Brooks. He was up in arms instantly, sniffing possible battle like an old war horse, and
insisting that he must go home at once. Heaven only
knows what he expected to do when he got there; in his
heart I think that he only longed for the excitement of seeing America at war. Having always maintained that the

soldier represented the highest type of manly virtue and that there were worse things than war, he was in a perfect fret to get back to see his country buckling on its armor. His favorite characters in fiction were all fighting men, either in his beloved Scott's novels or the heroic poems of Aytoun. He knew all of his *Scottish Cavaliers* by heart and had made me learn them too, so that after the United States had declared war on Spain he liked me to come down to breakfast reciting "News of battle! — news of battle! Hark! 'tis ringing down the street," on the theory that if he kept rubbing it in, I too might develop the proper martial spirit. He insisted that at heart all women were sentimental fools subject to every known sloppy emotion.

When it came to going home, I was the only thorn in his side, for his translation was finished and he was as nearly at loose ends as he ever permitted himself to be. I was a real obstacle, however, for as a specimen of a perfect lady I had not jelled to his satisfaction. The answer seemed to be to leave me behind for further culture. He had had this in mind for some time, as he had been planning a spring trip to Greece, but now, with the imperative urge to go home upon him, he was not a man to brook delay. His faith in the convent-bred woman being only second to his admiration for the martial man, it was decided that I should be left in a Catholic convent for further polishing. He consulted Mlle. Moynier who recommended the Convent of the Sacré Coeur, and, as my mother had gone there as a little girl, it was felt that it was highly appropriate and that she would

be sure to approve. Uncle Brooks was completely satisfied
with this reasoning — for according to his ideas all con-
vents were conservative, stable affairs and what had been
satisfactory fifty years before was bound to remain so still.

So he decided, and the very next day took me for an interview with the Mother Superior at the main building of
the convent on the boulevard des Invalides. We were received by the Reverend Mother in one of those immaculately clean but severe convent parlors calculated to strike
terror to the soul — it certainly did to mine, though Uncle
Brooks faced it like a lion. The Reverend Mother was a
formidable but withal eminently practical lady, for in spite
of her scrupulously correct manners, she proceeded to put
Uncle Brooks through an examination which would have
done credit to our Supreme Judicial Court. After inspect-
ing me with an eagle eye, she had to know in detail Uncle Brooks's financial status and then, through references
which she seemed prepared to check, whether his social position in his own country — a country about which she appeared blandly vague — was unassailable. Last but not
least she wondered whether I was well behaved and *séri-
euse*. When these points were covered to her satisfaction,
she agreed, pending further investigation, to accept me as a
pupil, although the interview was by no means over, as
then Uncle Brooks had to have his innings. He wanted to
enlarge on what he pleased to call my exceptional background and the sterling qualities of my Puritan inherit-
ance, only to be countered by the Reverend Mother who,

knowing little and caring less for the ramifications of Americans in general, and resenting the Puritanism in particular, fixed me with a suspicious eye and scathingly remarked, "Abigaeel — it is a Jewish name." My uncle was somewhat stumped by this shrewd remark but rose to it like a trout and tried to explain the fondness of the Puritans for biblical names and then waxing hot said, rather tartly, that I was one hundred per cent Anglo-Saxon, and that he did not wish to have me influenced by Catholic propaganda — to which her reply effectively closed the interview, as rising to her feet she remarked with great dignity, "But you say that she is a lady, so she will undoubtedly conform to our régime without scandal." Uncle Brooks realized that he was licked, and we departed leaving the Reverend Mother in complete control of the situation, and Uncle Brooks more than ever impressed with the superiority of the convent-bred woman. The next day. Aunt Evelyn went to the convent to inspect the quarters to be assigned to me, found them quite satisfactory, and when shortly afterwards we were notified that my application had been accepted, I at once entered the Convent and Aunt Evelyn and Uncle Brooks almost immediately sailed for home.

A letter which I received at about this time from my brother Charlie rather deflated the martial ardor that Uncle Brooks's warlike zeal had generated in me. Charlie had lately been elected Treasurer of Harvard College and I felt sure that his views represented the opinion of the ma-

jority of conservative down-to-earth Boston businessmen.
He wrote:

> We are on the verge of war. There is no great excite-
> ment outside of Washington and the business world does
> not anticipate any very serious or lasting struggle. Ev-
> erything goes on as usual and not even the Stock Market
> is seriously disturbed. I do not feel any anxiety lest the
> war should have an immediate disastrous result on our
> affairs, nor do I anticipate any ultimate results that will
> materially delay the financial recovery of the country.
> All of which goes to show that you can sleep as com-
> fortably as your convent bed allows without such ap-
> prehensions as a close association with Brooks, in the
> face of rumors of war, may have raised in your mind.

Needless to say my mind was completely befuddled
when confronted first by the mysticism of the Catholic
religion, and then by the diametrically opposite schools of
thought on the subject of the war from the two men on
whose judgment I most relied. Uncle Brooks's romantic
fervor seemed suddenly silly in the light of Charlie's calm
and moderate estimate. What was the answer? Were the
soldiers or what Uncle Brooks pleased to call the "money-
changers" going to control our destinies, and was Uncle
Brooks merely a goose and not a prophet at all? I was
fond of him and he had drenched me with his ideas, but detached as I was from the world and plunged into a medieval atmosphere I really did not know whether I was
standing on my head or my heels. In this dilemma the
Church won out, and I became shortly so immersed in the

77

engrossing occupations of the new life that nothing outside the convent walls interested me very much.

The Mother House of the convent was a huge uninteresting building facing the Invalides on the boulevard of the same name. Its façade from the street was totally severe and undistinguished, but inside the severity was relieved by glimpses of a big garden behind, which stretched down to the rue de Varennes, and the charming old hôtel there that had been the original Mother House. Our building on the boulevard des Invalides was modern and entirely utilitarian. There was nothing even vaguely to suggest either leisure or comfort. It was a desert of long halls and passageways all with immaculately clean, waxed floors and all seemingly empty, so that at first one felt as if one were living in a species of nightmare. The occasional religious statues were of no help to a miserable girl who was coming down with the first symptoms of homesickness. My homesickness was short-lived but acute for the moment, a horrid combination of nausea, insomnia and nervous collapse. I even yearned for the dubious comfort of Uncle Brooks's sympathy, but I snapped out of my troubles quite quickly, for the nuns were extraordinarily kind and understanding and the new life was enormously exciting to an ingrowing New Englander like myself. The environment was bewildering, but somehow the nuns made one feel at home and the Grandes Pensionnaires, as the boarders were called, were a varied enough lot to suit any taste, even that of a hidebound Yankee.

There were about twenty of us Grandes Pensionnaires all of different ages, nationalities and social standings — a truly democratic bunch. There were Belgian, Russian, Spanish, English, Irish and South American girls, but with none could you become really intimate, as the Church frowned upon close friendships between women, and no two girls were allowed to be alone together, while even groups of three or four unaccompanied by an older chaperone were regarded with suspicion. This system, though irritating and confining, did make for a clique-free communal life. For exercise we walked rather solemnly in the garden — a half hour every morning and afternoon — but our walks were well supervised and it was only in the refectory at meals that we were supposed to relax. The rule was that at meals — when we "broke bread" — we must all be jolly together and indulge in something called "Delicious Gaiety," though it might just as well have been called "Holy Hilarity" or even "Imbecile Fun." What it amounted to was a great deal of giggling over nothing in particular. The nuns had the secret of "Delicious Gaiety" down to a fine point and could turn it on and off at will. Something silly would be said and then, as if at a signal, we would all begin to giggle and make ridiculous remarks about nothing at all. We felt that we were being witty and would laugh away sociably without really knowing why. The nuns showed a great deal of common sense in their management of the girls, for though "Delicious Gaiety" may have been vapid and inane, it also made for a minimum of friction, nothing being ever said that might have started disagreement or bad feeling.

The lessons were ineffective because no two girls had had the same amount of preparation in any given subject, but as most of them were there primarily to learn French, other subjects were of minor importance. We had good religious instruction, in which, though not obliged to, I gladly joined. To begin with, I merely thought that going to Sacred Studies would at least be an improvement over sewing alone in my room, but I soon became deeply interested and found that it helped me to follow the varied services in the chapel which I attended regularly with the other girls. In chapel we wore over our heads heavy black veils, which we used as shawls the rest of the time. They were a species of uniform. We went to mass every morning before breakfast and to vespers every afternoon. As I had entered the convent shortly before Holy Week I was soon hardened to long stretches on my knees. I loved it all. I had never before been accustomed to church services or religious instruction and that, combined with the lovely ritual of the Catholic Church and the spiritual outlook of the nuns and their renunciation of the world, utterly overcame my inherited Puritanism and no one was more devout than myself. This metamorphosis may have taken a couple of weeks.

On the practical side, life in the convent was simple and primitive. There were no luxuries or frills. Physical cleanliness was hard to come by. Every night one was handed a small jug of warm water which sufficed for washing needs.

But on Saturdays, if one so desired, one could be escorted to a nearby bathing establishment, where, still supervised by a lay attendant, one could take a hot bath. The tin tub would be lined with a sheet and you were offered a coarse cotton nightshirt in which you were to shroud yourself while taking your bath. It didn't make sense, but that was the rule. The ubiquitous attendant and the nightshirt were supposed to prevent you from contemplating your own corrupt body and, incidentally, from either enjoying your bath or getting yourself clean in the process. It was such a silly and exasperating performance that I seldom took advantage of the privilege, especially as no one seemed to care whether I did or not. There was no compulsion in the matter, no one ever checked up to see if you were clean or not. We were supposed to be old enough to look after ourselves in those matters, so that it became entirely a matter of personal taste. As I remember, none of the girls bothered much about baths; they weren't the fashion.

Food was adequate though tasteless and monotonous — gruel and stew — stew and gruel. It was obviously supposed to nourish you without unduly gratifying your appetite, all of which it did, but in Holy Week we dropped to starvation rations, and I was definitely very hungry. Service was nonexistent. The food was placed on the table by the lay sister in large containers and was served by the refectory mistress. There were never any second helpings and you were expected to eat up every morsel that was set before you. On the table would also be placed a large pan of hot water in which we would all rinse our one fork or spoon when we were through using them, after which we rolled them in our napkin and tucked them into a horn ring marked with our name. We had a fresh napkin once a week. It was expected that our plates would be practically clean when we had finished our meal and this was done by sopping up any lingering fragments with pieces of bread. This made washing simpler and prevented waste. To waste food at the Sacré Coeur was a sin. Our drinking water was of the plain Parisian variety, but it was fortified with a dash of sour red wine, either to discourage the germs or else to invigorate us sufficiently to be able to cope with them. The only direct result beyond the fact that we all stayed well was that it made the water quite unpalatable. The ordinary dairy products were only noticeable by their absence, but we thought our afternoon *Goutées* absolutely delicious — good bread and hard chocolate eaten to the fatuous giggles of "Delicious Gaiety."

We exercised in the garden both morning and afternoon, if you can consider that short turns up and down the paths accompanied by a nun could be called exercise. It was explained to us that children could run and play but that we were young ladies and must observe the conventions. Once a week, Mlle. Moynier, my old governess from the rue de Verneuil, would come and chaperone me on my "afternoon out." On these festive occasions we always ended up for tea at the apartment of Miss Augusta Thorndike, who had been a friend of my family's and who was a lovely warm-hearted expatriate. Mlle. Moynier would leave me there and Miss Thorndike would send me back after filling me up with all the confections that I liked best, especially marrons glacées and chocolate éclairs, for it was not surprising that the convent fare made one frantic for sweets. Mlle. Moynier and I also had fun ordering dresses for my "coming out" which was due for the next season. On 'my mother's advice, we went to Worth where she was known — supplemented by Rouff who was favored by Uncle Brooks. Mlle. Moynier's French thrift and wordly acumen stood me in good stead on these expeditions, for life in the convent had deadened all my sense as to the value of money, while a handsome letter of credit was an added temptation.

With May came the news of the Battle of Manila Bay and my excitement was such, when the details finally were known, that I mustered up courage to ask the Reverend Mother if I could, in honor of the victory, stage a little celebration some evening in the refectory. As at that time the two Spanish pupils had already left, she did not think that it could be offensive to any of the others, entirely forgetting that we had a couple of South Americans with us who might not be at all sympathetic. That, however, did not bother her, as she vaguely classed us all together as Americans and so, probable compatriots. Her only stipulation was as to the time for this party and the promise that we would not make any unseemly noise, but she made the welcome concession of letting me provide all the cake and candy that I wanted. Thanks to this the party was a huge success. It was held in the refectory at the usual supper hour, "Delicious Gaiety" was turned on at full blast, while the South American girls aligned themselves under the Stars and Stripes with no visible compunction. Most of them never saw a newspaper from one week's end to the other and really did not know what it was all about, as the convent did not run a course on "Current Events," but they were starved for sweets and for any excitement and were so enthusiastic over the refreshments that it seemed as if they could never get enough. The thoughtful Mlle. Moynier had not only provided plenty of food but little American flags for everyone so that there should be no mistake as to our loyalties, and I even made a speech in my best French. I lauded the exploits of the American Navy in Manila Bay, but that fell rather flat as few knew where Manila Bay was or how revolutionary our victory had been. When the party was over, not a crumb of cake or morsel of candy was left and I quite complacently felt that I had fittingly upheld the honor of my country in a foreign land.

That party was an appropriate climax to my convent life, as shortly after that the girls began to scatter for the summer and I realized that the time had come for me to make some plan for myself. My mother had always brought me up on the simple slogan of "Use your own judgment, my dear," and, with a touching faith in that judgment and in my native common sense, had written to me to get myself a steamer ticket and come home when I was ready. I did not feel like coming home at that moment, for Uncle Henry with the Donald Camerons and the John Hays had taken a large country house in England for the summer and he had invited me to come over and visit him, which was a chance that I was not going to miss. So I made my plans accordingly, wrote Uncle Henry when I would arrive at Dover, collected my new dresses, said a sad good-bye to Miss Thorndike and the Sacré Coeur and, with the faithful Mlle. Moynier to see me off, left by the boat train for England and Uncle Henry.

"An architectural anomaly" — the house of
Mrs. Homans's father, John Adams, on Mt. Wollaston
in Quincy, Massachusetts.

The Old House in Quincy, Massachusetts, became
Brooks Adams's permanent home.

Below: The garden of the Old House showing the
library. *Courtesy The Adams National Historic Site,
National Parks Service, Department of the Interior.*

Charles Francis Adams at Harvard.
Courtesy Harvard University Archives.

John Adams about the time of his graduation
from Harvard in 1853.

Henry Adams at the time of his graduation from Harvard in 1858. *Courtesy Harvard University Archives.*

Brooks Adams while he was in school in England in the 1860's.

Brooks Adams at Harvard (1866–70).

Abigail Adams in about 1895.

Surrenden Dering, the manor house in Kent where Abigail Adams
visited her Uncle Henry in the summer of 1898. Below: Part of the
"complicated caravanserai" at Surrenden Dering — left to right,
rear row, seated: John Hay, his son Clarence, Edith Hoyt, Helen
Hay; seated in front: Martha Cameron, Alice Hay; standing:
Senator James D. Cameron, Henry Adams, Spencer Eddy (a
secretary at the U.S. Legation), Adelbert S. (Del) Hay.

The Glades in Minot, Massachusetts —
"monumental relic of a past age."

Henry Adams from a drawing
by John Briggs Potter.

CHAPTER SEVEN

LEAVING the cloistered and spiritual life of the convent behind me, I plunged into a totally different existence, adult, social and of the world. I came prepared to make Uncle Henry a short visit on my way home, but I had such a good time that it did not take much urging to get me to stay on for over two months. Uncle Henry, unlike my mother, and luckily for me, did not approve of young women crossing the ocean alone. His suggestion was that

I should make myself at home with him until Uncle Brooks and Aunt Evelyn turned up again sometime in September. This arrangement suited me beautifully. On that July day of 1898, when I arrived from France, Uncle Henry met me on the dock at Dover and by a series of cross-country trains via the large town of Ashford we reached Pluckley and the manor house of Surrenden Dering that Uncle Henry and the Camerons had taken for the season as a country retreat for the Hays and the embassy staff.

Inexperienced as I was with English country life, Surrenden Dering struck me as a romantic dream of beauty — a great Elizabethan country house standing foursquare on its grassy terraces overlooking the Weald of Kent. The approach was along a wooded Kentish ridge and the house was complete with all the proper·appendages of courtyard, gardens, stables and a park full of deer. The house was singularly dignified and austere, for it had never been tampered with and had a proud self-satisfied look that defied criticism. The interior was in keeping with its general appearance: the rooms large, stately and formal without any intimate charm, but filled with handsome, ponderous and uncomfortable furniture and enlivened only by a variety of dull family portraits. The dining room was the best room in the house, facing the south, drenched with light and big enough to hold our large contingent in great comfort, but if you wanted to relax, you were rather put to it to find a cozy corner anywhere. Still it was summer and we did most of our relaxing out of doors where we usually had a long drawn out tea in the afternoons on one of the lower terraces. Those terraces were rather a snare, as, to reach the lower one by the direct route and scorning a flight of stone steps, one had to slide down a grassy bank that was quite as treacherous as ice, and if one's foot slipped one landed unceremoniously under the tea table. One day later in the summer I remember a Boston friend, Arthur Hill, coming to grief in just that way when making his first appearance as a guest, and I shall never forget the lovely unselfconscious way in which he picked himself up and greeted the assembled company. Upstairs in the house there were plenty of bedrooms but, to our American eyes, a very inadequate supply of bathrooms, so that the bathing facilities were eked out in true British fashion with Sitz baths and large jugs of hot water.

Luckily the house was comparatively empty when I arrived, for I was stupefied by the whole establishment. Besides Uncle Henry there were only Senator and Mrs. Cameron and their young daughter Martha, and two nieces of Mrs. Cameron's, Rosina and Annie Hoyt, who were not sisters but cousins in the numerous Sherman clan from which Mrs. Cameron and the rest sprang. The name of the house was a puzzler for everyone. "Dering" was the family name, but "Surrenden" was never explained satisfactorily. The younger secretaries at the embassy in London used to think it funny at times, as we were still at war with Spain, to forward mail to "Surrender Daring," Pluckless, Kent — but it only confused the literal-minded postmistress at

Pluckley, so that after she had made several complaints, the joke had to be frowned upon.

There was a continual flow of visitors through the house, particularly over the weekends. The Hays, of course, and their entourage were permanent, and that included their son Del and his much younger brother Clarence, with the two daughters, Helen and Alice, both out in society. With them was usually one of the secretaries, Spencer Eddy, and often one or more of the girls' English admirers. One of the regular visitors was Ralph Palmer, a friend of Uncle Henry's since Civil War days when he had been for so many years a secretary to his father in London. Palmer was a queer, cadaverous, charming old fellow, a mine of information on all things English and a delightful companion on our sightseeing trips around the countryside. Another old friend dating back to Uncle Henry's youth in Quincy was Mrs. Oswald Charlton who had been Mary Campbell, a Quincy girl, and both Uncle Henry and Uncle Brooks were devoted to her. She was still a lovely creature and great good company. Then came the more formal guests, the Morton Frewens, Helen Brice with her father the ex-Senator from New York and a near neighbor of Uncle Henry's at home, and, after them, the other Bryce — James, the author of *The American Commonwealth* who was later to be the British Ambassador in Washington. Another ex-American guest was the beautiful Mrs. George Curzon, who as Mary Leiter had been one of Uncle Henry's most cherished breakfast-table intimates in Washington before her marriage. A few

months after our meeting at Surrenden, Curzon was made
Lord Curzon of Kedleston and the next year became Vice-
roy of India. Mrs. Curzon had a little girl along, so that
with the two sons of the Michael Herberts — another Eng-
lishman with an American wife — there was quite a nurs-
ery of children to help fill the big house. So it went, and
as a neighbor, there was the Poet Laureate, Alfred Austin,
who would come over from his home at Swinford Old
Manor to pay his respects to Mr. Hay, whom he seemed to
regard as a fellow Poet Laureate somewhat to Mr. Hay's
annoyance, for, in spite of his genial good humor he was
always reluctant to have his *Pike County Ballads* taken
too seriously — and he found Mr. Austin's manner both
oppressively laudatory and portentous.

The country around Surrenden was lovely and we were
blessed all through the summer with the most divine
weather in which to enjoy it. There were available walks
in every direction and like Jane Austen's Mrs. Elton we did
a good deal of "exploring" — not perhaps in a barouche
landau as in *Emma*, but in something not very dissimilar.
Uncle Henry, with his bird-dog instinct for history and human relics, smelled out a number of old parish churches in
the immediate neighborhood which were well worth a visit,
in addition to the more spectacular sights such as Penshurst,
Ightham Mote and Hever Castle — the last two sacred to
the stormy memory of Anne Boleyn. At that time both of
those houses were unrestored and delightfully dilapidated,
and as there were no other tourists around to vex us we

were allowed to poke about them at will, with Uncle Henry supplying all the historical information. Farther afield were Rochester and Canterbury which involved all-day trips by a series of slow cross-country railroad trains and were the greater fun for all the complications. Our sightseeing contingent usually consisted of the two Hoyt girls, the two Hay girls, and myself, with Uncle Henry at his most genial and academic best as guide and teacher. At home, although there was no tennis court, no bowling green and no river, the days were never long enough, for guests were always coming or going and in the long summer afternoons we spent a great deal of time drinking tea on the lower terrace under the shade of the trees. For these occasions we females dressed up in thin summer dresses and topped them with big picture hats.

That energetic red-blooded American, Senator Cameron, scorning tea and perhaps all things English, had managed to produce from somewhere a pair of long-tailed trotting horses and a buggy with which he amused himself by tearing around the staid Kentish countryside and frightening the ponderous native work horses into all sorts of cavorting. He was very kind to me and used often to take me with him and we certainly covered an enormous amount of country at top speed. As he often got lost and was impatient of asking questions, these expeditions were frequently quite exciting. The Senator had also had sent over from the States a large consignment of his favorite fruits and vegetables, the enjoyment of which he did not want to miss by passing a season away from home. These included, among other delicacies, not only corn but the humble watermelon, neither of which our rather prim and conventional British cook had ever seen before. She struggled fairly successfully with the corn, although she deplored the manner in which, as she said, it was "gnawed" at the table, but the watermelons defeated her, for she boiled them and served them as a horrible gelatinous pulp. Even the Senator, who really was a good sport at heart, had to laugh, and the disgruntled cook redeemed herself by proving to be quite a competent hand at sugared sweet potatoes. Senator Cameron was not a conversationalist nor could he fit himself easily into the lazy alien life of an English country house existence; he would bury himself in the newspapers, many of which, pertaining to his local Pennsylvania interests, he had sent over from America, and he took his wild drives, but after that he was rather at a loss. He wasn't interested in chitchat and even eschewed politics as a conversational gambit. As for Uncle Henry's philosophical whimsical musings, he mistrusted them profoundly. He was not often open or companionable, but sometimes an unexpected cordiality would break down the crust of shyness in which his queer self-distrust wrapped him and he would burst out into real volubility and even affection. He was in many ways a very intriguing character.

Uncle Henry, as well as Senator Cameron, went in for horseflesh, but Uncle Henry's venture was more restrained. He hired two chubby brown ponies and with Martha Cameron on a leading rein would ride almost every day. Martha was a pretty little girl about eleven years old with a straight nose, blue eyes and the fattest of yellow pigtails. Of the older ladies I can hardly speak adequately for I regarded them with proper awe.

Mrs. Don Cameron was on the whole the most socially competent woman that I had ever met. With perfect self-confidence she could tackle any situation and appear to enjoy it. She was not perhaps strictly beautiful, but she was such a mass of style and had such complete self-assurance that she always gave the appearance of beauty and she gave everyone a good time when she set out to please. She was not only the hostess for this big and complicated caravanserai, but she ran it as well, and I doubt if many details escaped her eagle eye. Of course there was the usual imposing housekeeper who was supposed to superintend everything, but no proper English lady would let it go at that, and neither did Mrs. Cameron, though she did it all with a minimum of fuss and feathers. She checked on all the expenditures and knew minutely what was going on, for there was a good deal of the Yankee in her. She never discussed the below-stairs problems except with Mrs. Charlton, for Mrs. Charlton — after many years in England on pretty short commons — had been able to combine the humorous qualities of the American with the caste-ridden insight of the English housewife. When those two got together talking over the intricacies of the English domestic system, it was the greatest fun in the world and made the tedious business of running a big establishment seem like some huge joke. Mrs. Cameron, while looking over the bills, would ask Mrs. Charlton, "What percentage of graft is considered legitimate in a house of this size, for I refuse to be bothered with it unless it is all out of scale?" — and then Mrs. Charlton would start in on the ridiculous side of some of the hard and fast unwritten domestic usages which had to be considered, and we would all end up perfectly satisfied that Surrenden was worth the rake-off no matter what the scale. It gave you a pleasant cozy feeling that you were all having a good time together.

Mrs. Hay was different again. She was a most majestic-appearing person with an alarming exterior but a warm heart. She was kind, generous, unpretentious and completely unselfconscious, and while I am sure that she was thoroughly efficient in running the embassy, I doubt if she would have considered the mechanics of it as in the least humorous. Though she made no pretense of being an intellectual, she had a wonderful fund of common sense and nothing escaped her. She was a big woman with very handsome features and a most lovely smile. She was utterly devoted to her family and I am sure that they all depended on her as a tower of strength. One became very fond and admiring of Mrs. Hay.

Helen the oldest daughter was more like her father, small, witty, fascinating looking and definitely an intellectual. She was even then starting to write poetry, although her young admirers were keeping her pretty busy through that summer. Alice, her younger sister, was much like her mother in both looks and temperament, and like her was warm-hearted and sympathetic, with a lovely convivial streak which made her great fun. Adelbert, the oldest son, was then a great big fellow of much promise in the class of '98 at Yale. And Clarence the youngest was perhaps thirteen.

Of Mr. Hay I have not spoken because it seemed to me to be none of my business to analyze him. He was the closest possible friend to Uncle Henry, and I accepted him, as I did my uncle, as a being apart. As I saw him he was invariably kind and most considerate — a little remote and detached from everyday life, but with a lighthearted wit and conviviality which made him the best of good company. But underneath his facile manners one sensed a nervous tension that plagued him continually and prevented him from really enjoying his post in England, which at that time must have been a most agreeable one. He personally was well liked, and the respect for the United States which the recent exploits of our Navy had produced, made the international atmosphere, for the moment, particularly friendly.

Suddenly, one evening in August, there came what to me was stunning news. President McKinley had offered Mr. Hay the Secretaryship of State in his Cabinet. To my intense surprise the reaction to this announcement from Mr. Hay's devoted circle at Surrenden was distinctly apathetic. Not only did no one seem excited, but worse, no one seemed even pleased. This indifference to what seemed to me a great honor puzzled me enormously, till from the conversation it dawned on me that Mr. Hay was tired and that he was more than a little reluctant to take on further responsibility, while at the same time doubting his ability to cope with the increased nervous strain involved in accepting the promotion. As I listened to the discussion it became clear that they all agreed on one point — either Mr. Hay must accept the President's offer or resign from the government, for as Uncle Henry rather sadly put it, "No serious statesman can accept a favor and refuse a service." It was somehow all in the day's work for a government official — you either accepted or you got out — it was as simple as that. In this case, Mr. Hay accepted.

Surrenden lost its charm after that dramatic touch. It was no longer a country retreat and a playground — the Hays were packing up and going home — the fun was over and one felt decidedly flat. The arrival of Uncle Brooks and Aunt Evelyn, who, since Paris, had been at home and come out again, did not add much to the gaiety of nations, although Uncle Brooks was in remarkably good form — pleased with the war, which was then ending, pleased with the French translation of his *Civilization and Decay*, and, though still convinced that the world was going to the devil, thinking that with a few more wars it might keep going at least until he was dead. But the time to leave had come, and by the middle of September everyone was scattering. Uncle Henry was going north to visit some old friends, the Camerons were leaving for Paris before going home, and Uncle Brooks and Aunt Evelyn with me in tow were headed for Boston. I had been away for nearly a year, had had a wonderfully interesting winter, followed by a superlative summer — but in the process I had lost touch with Boston, and neither my French winter nor my English summer were the right preparation for "coming out" in Boston society which was to be my next move.

CHAPTER EIGHT

C OMING OUT in Boston at the end of the century was a pretty momentous affair. It was not only the end of the century, but the end of a social era as well, and society, as such, was never again quite so solemn or important. Coming out then was a time-consuming process, and you could not very well combine being a debutante with either college work or the responsibilities of a job. As a matter of fact, there were very few jobs available for girls at that time; they had no training, and unless your family were definitely hard up, it was felt that you had no business to take the bread out of some really poor girl's mouth. Higher education was not thought very desirable; it was all very well if a girl was a bluestocking and sincerely yearned for college, but in that case it was apt to mean that the girl would be a social pill anyhow and might as well go her own way. The general feeling among the mothers was that you were only young once and had better make hay while the sun shone. Of course they complacently overlooked the fact that when you were young was the only time when you could prepare yourself for a career, short of selling hats or being a companion to some elderly relation. For me college was definitely out, as my family not only did not encourage the idea, but my Parisian winter had not fitted me for any college board examinations. With my sketchy education it would have taken me a full year of hard work to prepare for them. In any case, I had no intention of following any line but the most obvious and conventional one. But if I were unfitted for college, I was equally unfitted for an introduction to Boston society. The "convent-bred woman" that Uncle Brooks had hoped he was training me to be was not at all the type to be successful on the dance floor. To be a belle one should have stayed at home, gone to the essential Friday and Saturday evening dancing classes — a heritage from Mr. Papanti — known the right boys and been intimate with the right girls. A year in Europe was hardly the correct preparation for bucking the competition of a rather superlative group of debutantes. Fortunately for me they were a very friendly set and took me back into their midst as cozily as if I had never been away. That included election into the year's Sewing Circle, and an invitation to join one of the many lunch clubs. The girls couldn't have been nicer; the real trouble was with the young men. The young men were mostly college boys with the exception of freshmen, who were considered too immature. Those in the graduate schools or who had already started in business or a profession were spoken of as older men. Harvard was such a reservoir of men that the students felt their oats a little and were not prepared, when there were so many charming girls around, to bother much about unfamiliar females with whom it might be an effort to get acquainted. I was also slightly hampered in a materialistic way by the fact that my family had not yet recovered their financial equilibrium and were reluctant to spend any money in entertaining for my benefit, so that not even a dinner was given in my honor. Still that deprivation had its rosy side, for I was at least spared having a tea put on for my introduction. Teas were ghastly affairs as far as entertainment was concerned, but a few dinners would have been a help. Boys did not come to teas, which were invented so that the debutante might be presented to her mother's, aunts' and grandmother's friends, and the plaudits of those matrons were about all the satisfaction that these entertainments could offer. Mercifully teas were beginning to go out of fashion in my day, for they meant a grueling afternoon for a poor "bud." One was expected to be endlessly polite while dressed much too elaborately in an overheated and overcrowded house. If you were favored with an invitation to "pour," you were condemned to sit at one end of the dining-room table and dispense whatever beverage had its headquarters there.

Our clothes, which covered us from our chins to our heels, did have a certain style which has now completely vanished, but they were hideously uncomfortable and horribly cumbersome, and an afternoon imprisoned in one of those high-necked and long-sleeved atrocities was a truly formidable experience. I don't remember that anything stronger than tea or coffee was ever served, although a bowl of punch might have been lurking around somewhere. The food consisted of enormous quantities of fantastic sandwiches cut in every kind of grotesque shape, and masses of delicious little cakes and candies. Occasionally an older man of the father or grandfather vintage would appear momentarily, but as I have said, it was rare that any young man would dare to show his face. After all, there was no room to dance in or music to dance to, so why come?

Real dances were a different thing altogether. The small house dances could be great fun: they were informal and casual and if you did not know all the boys your hostess would see that you were introduced, while at the same time there was no great stigma attached to being an occasional wallflower. Dinner dances in private houses were very swank, rather formal and definitely sophisticated. There would be a few of them each season in the bigger houses, some of which even boasted a ballroom, and there would then be a cotillion and something rather extra in the way of favors. The real thrills came from the Assemblies, two of which were held each season in the biggest and most fashionable of the hotels. There one would wear one's best bib and tucker and would be escorted by an usher to curtsy to an imposing line of Patronesses some of whom would be sporting tiaras and suchlike decorations. As these were the highlights of the season only a few debutantes were invited, while Harvard freshmen were rigorously excluded. At the two Assemblies there was always a cotillion, and if you went to one without a cotillion and supper partner already secured, you were decidedly out of luck.

Cotillions had a certain rather stately quality that lent a dance a good deal of dignity. Chairs were arranged around the ballroom and tied together by twos. Each lady was given a number by the leader of the cotillion, who, I am sure, always reserved the choicest seats for his favorite ladies. His job it was to direct the whole affair. He would call out the first four or five couples, give them each a favor, after which they would dance off — and it was always a waltz that they danced to — and then they would separate and each man would give his favor to whomever of the opposite sex he happened to fancy. Then these new couples would dance and then return to their seats to wait, while the next set of couples went out and took the floor. It made the dancing delightful for those who were frequently favored, and the watching rather dreadful for those who were not taken out. It was wonderful when you saw a friend coming toward you with a favor, but agonizing when you saw him hesitate, change his mind and give it to someone else. The leader of the cotillion would keep his eye on the couples that were dancing and would clap his hands and send them back to their seats when he thought that they had had the floor long enough. If you did go to a cotillion without a partner there was always the chance that you might pick one up, for the men were quite as anxious as the girls to have a seat on the dance floor, and although these last-minute arrangements were merely face-saving, they were better than nothing. If no one turned up, you were lost and had to retire to the dressing room and from there maneuver yourself — unseen if possible — to one of those respectable vehicles, a Kenny and Clark cab, and so get yourself home. Like all dances since the world began, it was heaven if you had a good time but hell if you didn't. To be "stuck" for dance after dance was the most mortifying thing in the world. No wonder that my mother said that dances were a part of my education. With cotillions, even when properly supplied with a partner, the kind of a time that you had was horribly conspicuous. You either had plenty of favors given you, which you could stuff under your chair with studied nonchalance, or else you only had a meager one or two, which you could neither conceal nor exploit. It was thrilling to leave a ballroom dripping with favors, but equally upsetting to walk out with nothing to show for your charms but perhaps one conspicuous little gewgaw. The prettiest favors and the most decorative were broad bands of ribbon caught together by some shiny tinsel, which you could drape over your shoulder and which were pleasantly striking both for men and women. One always tried to keep up appearances by announcing the next day that "it" had been great fun, or else receive such consolation as I sometimes got from my mother, who, as she unlaced my dress (a thing that one could not do one's self without apoplexy), noticing my one lonely scalp would say, "No matter, my dear, it is all a part of your education." Somehow that simple philosophy was not much comfort to a would-be belle.

Our evening dresses were lovely — satin or silk with tulle ruffles which swung out delightfully when one danced. These tulle ruffles would tear at the slightest provocation, but when they started to rip no pretense was ever made to save them and they were ruthlessly torn off and poked under the nearest chair. To lose your tulle ruffles was a sign that you were having a good time, and if they came through the evening intact it rather marked you as being a pill. Next day some "little woman" would appear at your house to sew on a fresh set of ruffles so that your damaged dress might be ready for the next fray.

There were other subscription dances besides the Assemblies, like the "Cheap and Hungries," but they were held in an inferior hall with a correspondingly meager supper. Dinners were apt to be very pleasant and usually preceded the big balls, and with them there was always the excitement of wondering who would "take you in" and who would talk to you after dinner. At all the formal dinners the men found little envelopes waiting for them on the hall table, inside which would be the name of the lady whom they were to escort in to dinner. And when I say "escort" I mean just that, for they offered you their arm and you filed in to dinner in procession. After dinner the proceedings were not so simple, as at the first sound of approaching male voices the close female groups would scatter and each girl try to isolate herself in some strategic position near an empty seat hoping that some unsuspecting male would see it and come to rest there. That was all very well, but sometimes you were left with an empty seat and no occupant and then your hostess had to come to your rescue leaving you covered with confusion. Though not shy I was unused to seeing boys naturally, and long association with Uncle Brooks was not conducive to giving me a light touch with Harvard undergraduates, but as my mother said, it was all part of my education and not to be taken too seriously. My mother was a true lady of the old school, and although she had rigid ideas on deportment she did not follow me up too closely. One of her great slogans when I would come to her for advice was, "You must use your own judgment, my dear." Of course it went without saying that ladies never crossed their legs in public: you could cross your ankles but nothing more, neither could you ar-·range your hair or touch your face once you had left the shelter of the dressing room, while to apply powder or lipstick was unthinkable. My mother expected me to look after myself about getting home, although when I arrived I had to wake her up so that she would know that I was safely back, and it was then that she would unlace my dress for me and perhaps give me a little wise advice if she thought necessary. I only hope that she popped off again to sleep easily.

The purely female side of coming out was naturally less exciting. Wednesdays were customarily devoted to Sewing Circles, while lunch clubs were tucked in on any old day except Fridays, which then, as now, were sacred to the Symphony Concerts. Sewing Circles were a legacy from an earlier period when sewing for the poor was a recognized charity and could be properly diluted with a little mild conviviality, but in my time they were on their last legs as serious charitable affairs. They still went on, but only as social occasions. As some scoffer put it, a Sewing Circle was only to "gabble, gobble, gossip and git." I never gave my Sewing Circle a fair trial as I resigned early, but at one of the first meetings that I did attend, a huge straw hamper was brought in and we were all allotted some specific project to work on, and were expected to pitch in and do our stint. Perhaps that one meeting was enough for me, for I do not remember ever seeing that hamper again. Society was staging a mild form of social revolution at the turn of the century, of which abandoning the Sewing Circle hamper was a symptom. The women were then beginning to take the bit in their teeth and substitute for sewing a new career of raising money and seeing to it that it was well spent.

At that time there developed an amazing set of older women who organized committees of every description, educated the younger women, and worked them in as junior members. Nothing daunted them, and these energetic and able women tackled all the problems of family life as well as the training of hospital nurses, the rehabilitation of prisoners, the protection and recreation of children, and regulation of the saloons. It was the beginning of modern organized charity and it was done quietly by these remarkable Boston women who put their whole hearts into it. Not only did they give material help but with it they gave a lot of sound advice, and they took the time and energy to establish friendly personal relations with those whom they served, so that in time they built up an enduring connection. My mother was not one of these imaginative and pioneering women, so that I did not figure among the public-spirited recruits, nor did many of the younger girls, for again the cry was that we were only young once and must be spared the more seamy side of life.

Instead our social duties involved "calls," which had to be taken mighty seriously. A call on your hostess within a week was considered *de rigueur* after you had been to a dinner, while a little more latitude was allowed after a dance. To go calling, one wore a long dress which was held up with one hand to prevent its dragging in the dust, clean white kid gloves, and carried a card case. Usually no one would be at home so that you could accomplish a good deal in an afternoon. Sporting Sunday house parties had not developed for the young. We did go occasionally to a country dinner and dance at the Wayside Inn at Sudbury, but those would be jolly informal affairs where one wore short dresses and did a good deal of innocent romping. Adventurous expeditions to the remote Siberian wilds of New Hampshire and Vermont were considered more suitable for the younger married set.

At the end of the season I wrote quite frankly in my diary that though I had not been a belle I had had a good enough time and that at least what success I had had was entirely on my own merits, since no one had felt under any obligation to speak to me unless they wanted to. That seems like an honest appraisal. With Ash Wednesday the Boston season ended and I went down to Washington for a rather quiet visit with Uncle Henry, going down again later with my mother for my brother Charlie's wedding to Frances Lovering, by which time Uncle Henry had gone to Europe. Summer at the Glades Club, as it then was, followed — swimming, sailing and tennis — after which I plunged into my second season. This time I was under a real handicap, for my family were still feeling poor and it was decided that we must rent the Boston house and that my brother George, my brother Arthur (who was in college), my mother and I should pass the winter in Quincy. That proved to be a rigorous experience. The Quincy house was completely unfitted to be a winter residence, or if it had been adequate once, it had since degenerated badly. The furnace was so old-fashioned that it would not give enough hot air to even mildly temper the Arctic air of our baronial front hall. We would bolt from room to room clinging to open fires and longing for bed and a hot-water bottle, while the plumbing would freeze at the slightest provocation. Added to these material troubles, my oldest brother George was taken sick with pleurisy early in February and was for a while desperately ill. He improved slightly as time went on but he was never well again and died the following July. That was a dreary time, but my mother kept repeating her favorite war cry that one was only young once and insisted that I should keep not only what engagements I already had but accept any future ones that came my way.

Quincy at best was not a convenient jumping-off place

for social life in Boston. The trip to town meant packing up a trunk — for no bag could hold your ball dress, evening wrap and all the other accessories — and then checking the wretched thing in by train and having it loaded onto a cab at the other end. I used to pass the night with some kind friend or relation, but it was a tiresome business and rather took the joy out of life. Then too it was not easy in Quincy to get someone to repair the ravages of a good party, and even if you did find a "little woman" she had to be transported back and forth to her home, while if you did the job yourself it was usually a mess.

House parties in the country were rare but very exciting. As I was a rider, and on the outer fringes of the sporting set, I went to several down at Myopia where we did a lot of riding, dancing and playing cards. Bridge was just coming in but it had not become a great gambling game, nor was anyone very expert at it. Those weekends were merciful escapes from Boston Sundays which had enough of the Puritan atmosphere left to make them rather dreary affairs, nor was a quiet Sunday at Quincy any improvement. Our sporting life consisted of skating, when the erratic New England climate made ice available, or snow-shoeing when that was possible. River skating was wonderful and to skate for miles down the Sudbury or the Charles was, though exhausting, the best of fun, while even an afternoon on Hammond's Pond in Chestnut Hill, though tamer, was not to be sneezed at.

My energetic and unaccountable Uncle Charles had sev-

eral years before bought a large country estate in Lincoln
looking out on Fairhaven Bay of the Sudbury River, and
later I passed many happy weekends out there. In his fine
inscrutable way he had acquired it all unbeknownst to his
family while they were abroad, and was perfectly delighted with himself for his enterprise in so doing. He said
that he had outgrown Quincy and that he left it without a
moment's regret. The Lincoln place he had acquired from
a friend who had aimed at becoming a country gentleman
only to discover too late that his family found Lincoln in-
tolerably lonely and devastatingly hot in summer. Nothing
of that nature bothered Uncle Charles and he took endless
satisfaction in his new plaything, finding fresh interests and
delights on every side. He had jumped at the chance to
pull up stakes and leave Quincy before, as he put it, he was
too old to enjoy a change of scene. He had made the decision at a moment's notice but it was a wise one and in keeping with his enthusiastic vitality. Quincy was becoming
increasingly suburban and he would never have been contented there indefinitely. Uncle Charles reveled in new
surroundings, for later, after a winter spent in a hired house
in Washington, he sold his house in Boston and bought one
in Washington which he proceeded to redecorate according
to his own fancy. As he wrote in his autobiography, he had
tried Boston society drunk and he had tried it sober, and
drunk or sober there was nothing in it. Washington, he
said, would provide new and interesting people. Uncle
Henry, in his quiet retreat on H Street, chuckled when he

heard this, and murmured that new and interesting people were just the stimulant that he was trying to avoid. The two brothers were very friendly but not at all intimate or intellectually sympathetic and living in the same city did not bring them any closer together than had their earlier life in Quincy.

Uncle Brooks in the meantime had been shuttling from one continent to another working on trade routes and financial drifts. He was in India one winter studying its financial problems, and yet another winter found him in Syria hotfoot on the trail of a gentleman called Tiglath-Pileser, a man after Uncle Brooks's own heart, for history relates that he spent his life (about 1100 B.C.) in waging continuous warfare, mostly in defending his trade routes. There were several Tiglath-Pilesers and Brooks liked them all. Uncle Brooks would come back to Quincy for the summers all steamed up over what he had discovered and would at once busy himself with his writing. He was never very peaceful or relaxed. During the summers I would see both my aunt and uncle all the time and I would take long drives with Uncle Brooks and try to absorb some of the details of medieval finance and the great significance of trade routes that he tried to instill in me. Once I complained to my Aunt Evelyn that I thought that Uncle Brooks fully expected to run into a caravan some day on Milton Hill, and my aunt laughed and told me how when they were in Syria and were planning a trip to the ruins of the Krak des Chevaliers, Uncle Brooks had suddenly said in his most serious tone, "Very well, Evelyn, you go and order the camels."

After two winters my social efforts as a "bud" were definitely over, for the next winter I spent with my mother in Rome. My oldest brother had died and she wanted to get away for a while. Though in many ways I had an interesting and rewarding time, I missed my independence, for looking after a parent is a confining occupation, as one had to be continually the fizz in the champagne, and constant sightseeing is hard on the young. I've no doubt that it was all a part of my education — my mother said so at any rate — but I yearned to get out on my own away from all restraints. I did take desultory Italian lessons and honestly tried to make the most of my opportunities, but I was glad when spring came and we went off on a tour around Italy before going home. I remember one mortifying episode on that trip. It was in a train going to Florence, and the only other occupant of the carriage was a most resplendent Italian naval officer, magnificent in gold braid. Somewhat to my surprise this gorgeous being made some obvious excuse to pick my acquaintance, and introduced himself by offering me his card, and explaining that he was *Comandante* of a certain battleship. That sounded pretty good to me and he began laying himself out to be agreeable and telling me about a book that he had written, *La Guerra in Mare*, which he considered superior to our Captain Mahan's book on the same subject. At point my mother, feeling that he was perhaps being a little fresh with me and wishing to give me some consequence, threw in the dreadful remark that I was a descendant of American presidents. The poor bewildered man, not being in the least conversant with American history, at once arose, bowed stiffly from the waist, and said, "It is indeed a privilege to meet the Honorable Miss McKinley." It was no use going into explanations, and I was far too dumfounded to even try — I could only giggle and hope that my mother would let it go at that.

June found us at home again just in time for the perennial excitement of attending Harvard Commencement. I may be speaking somewhat sarcastically when I describe Commencement as exciting, but I always went and I always enjoyed it. My brother was Treasurer of the University and, as my father had also been a Fellow, I felt a proprietary interest in the institution, and with several of my friends graduating at that time the interest was personal as well. Commencement was an all-day affair and toward the end of June the weather was apt to be hot, but in spite of these drawbacks I considered it a privilege to go and never missed an opportunity.

My father and his brother Charles made at least two trips to the Glades in their youth, and despite its fallen estate, my ultra-respectable and straitlaced grandfather, Charles Francis Adams, Sr., took it in one summer, for he loved the sea quite as much as his two older sons did.

When my father and his brother made their first excursion to the Glades it was still a modest boardinghouse, but by their second visit it had begun to go downhill, and Uncle Charles later confessed with glee that he had spent most of his time there playing penny poker. It was shortly after the end of the Civil War that the various Glades ventures finally went on the rocks for good, and the whole place was put up for sale. By great good luck there were, at that time, a group of gentlemen looking for a summer playground for themselves and their families and they bought the whole point, forming a club to hold the property. That arrangement worked most happily for a time, but by 1880 two of the members wished to retire and sell their shares. It was then that my father and his brother Charles came into the picture. By a curious coincidence very characteristic of their independent actions, each bought into the Glades Club without the other's knowing anything about it and neither heard of the other's intention until it was all settled. My father took over the upper apartment in the big Ell, while Uncle Charles shared a nearby cottage with the Robert Codman family. Later he enlarged it to make himself more comfortable, and for good measure built a preposterous tower at one end which

CHAPTER NINE

THE STORY of the family would be incomplete without a chapter on the Glades. The Glades stands on a stark neck of land jutting out into Massachusetts Bay, halfway between Boston and Plymouth, and only saved from the fury of the winter storms by its fringes of protecting rocks and outer ledges. Here on the Glades point are the first rocks north of Plymouth, which perhaps represent the "stern and rock-bound coast" described so dramatically in the well-known poem. Be that as it may, the point or points — for there are two — lie in the township of Scituate and are a mile distant from Minot's Ledge Lighthouse which rises from the ocean in barren grandeur directly to the north. Though now reduced to the rating of a third-class light, Minot's was once a vital landfall for ships making Boston Harbor, for it marked a particularly vicious sunken reef as well as the outer edge of a line of ledges which had been an area responsible for many wrecks. The two points of the Glades property are connected by a short stony beach. Each point has its bulwarks of rocks to protect it from the ocean, but the land itself is almost nonexistent — merely a mixture of rock and swamp supporting only the hardiest vegetation. Away from the sea with its salt spray are some sheltered acres where trees have survived — a few oaks and some delightful stands of tupelos and the more exotic holly. The tupelos are a perfect almanac for marking the end of the summer season, for by the fifteenth of August they invariably show their first signs of autumn scarlet. The holly trees unfortunately grow beside the avenue and are so well known that they are continually being plundered by thoughtless trespassers. There is even enough arable land away from the sea on the second point to have tempted some tough New Englanders to try their hand there at a little farming. Their efforts were never very successful, but one hardy individual did hold on long enough to leave his name as a heritage — so we have Wattles and Wattles Beach. Wattles Beach, which separates

the two points, is the slender thread that is the G line to civilization, for over it runs our one availa the outer world, and unless the road across W we should be dependent on our legs or our boat portation. In summer we are comparatively s winter when a savage northeaster roars in from the first thought of all Glades proprietors in thei able homes is, Will Wattles Beach go out? for i means a big expense to build the road in again.

Why the place is called the Glades, no one plained. It seems a singularly inappropriate nam cel of land that is mostly rocks and certainly ha of trees. On the topographical maps what we k Glades is called Strawberry Point, but to speak c seems merely silly to those of us who spend t there and also to the natives of Scituate.

It all started in the late 1840's as a summer solid, square-built house. Why anyone in his could have conceived of such a venture I have derstood, for the only available transportation b hasset, which was the railroad terminal at that ti sailboat, and so therefore dependent on the wind, weather and tide.

As might have been predicted, the project wa cess, but when it failed another optimist took ov and enlarged it, only to come to grief once n the house gradually sank into a sporting retreat gambling establishment.

added considerably to the general architectural confusion.

As a result of all this, the Glades has been an important element in our family's life for almost one hundred years. It has been the beloved playground and sanctuary not only of my father and Uncle Charles but also of my three brothers — George, Charles and Arthur — and has continued as such for my children and grandchildren. My uncles Henry and Brooks do not come into the Glades picture at all, although Uncle Brooks was once induced to come down there for lunch, only to remark later, "Oh, that is the place where they all eat in the cellar." That rather hurt our feelings, perhaps because there was a decided ring of truth in it — for our communal dining room was below the level of the land on one side, though open to the sea on the other.

The Glades house, a sprawling monstrosity, was built at the extreme westernmost tip of the property, with a substantial fringe of land around it, which has since been so eaten into by the sea that now there is only room enough to drive a car along its eastern side, while the waves in winter sometimes batter at the kitchen windows. No human habitation short of a lighthouse could be more exposed or have a more tremendous sweep of sea view. The original building was soundly constructed on granite foundations, an uncompromising square mansion, while above its two stories were a couple of receding cupolas which gave it a gay wedding-cake appearance and enabled visitors to watch for incoming ships. Later two wings were added, a low one to the north and a huge three-story affair to the south, the basement of which was the enormous dining room described as a cellar by the critical Uncle Brooks. The dining room extended — quite unsupported — for the whole length of the ponderous structure. As an architectural phenomenon it is amazing, for though the wing is now slightly out of plumb, on the whole it has stood up remarkably well. With time the exterior of the house has sprouted piazzas and outside staircases, while inside it has developed bathrooms and individual kitchens — but it would take more than such minor details to alter the character of the building. These developments have been the work of several notably able and efficient women, who, as circumstances have arisen, have adapted the house to meet the needs of a changing society. In the beginning there were no bathrooms. The ocean was supposed to attend to that — and there was a communal kitchen in the basement to supply all the culinary services; but now every apartment has its own kitchen, dining room, and bathroom, while the huge basement dining room now has been taken over by a third generation of Adamses as a crude children's rumpus room. This great metamorphosis was caused by the Second World War when it became impossible to. staff the club house and every family had to be responsible for their own maintenance. My indomitable and efficient sister-in-law, Mrs. C. F. Adams III, first started the idea of separate kitchens which she did by taking a couple of the superfluous cell-like bedrooms and improvising them for their new functions. Once started, the idea spread like wildfire and soon stoves sprouted in spare bedrooms everywhere. It is much better this way, because the kitchen was always a horrid hole, hot, ill-ventilated and inhabited by all sorts of objectionable insects. The Glades should really now be preserved as a monumental relic of a past age, a perfect example of the now practically extinct early American summer hotel, complete with public rooms, acres of shingled roofs and enormous circling piazzas.

Why, over the years before the merciful advent of Dr. Augustus Thorndike, we did not all die of ptomaine poisoning from food prepared in that loathsome common kitchen is beyond me. He is a member of the club now and he took hold of our sanitation problem with a firm hand and revolutionized it. The women who were the "girls" of the Glades in the eighties and nineties used to refer to the kitchen with trumped-up nostalgia as the "dear old kitchen," but my memories of it are principally of the horrid swarms of flies that blackened the ceiling and that would hiss at you when you disturbed them like a lot of angry serpents. In fact, why the Glades or any of its inhabitants survived is a miracle, for before electricity was installed the whole place was lighted by kerosene oil lamps precariously balanced in wall brackets and liable to be blown down at any moment — while our clams which we considered particularly succulent were dug from the flats behind the house over which the sewerage was emptied at high tide. That has now been stopped by our Commissioner of Conservation Francis W. Sargent, who before that was the Commissioner of Fisheries and so was entitled by his authority, and also as a member of the Glades family, to deprive us of our clams.

At the time when my father and my Uncle Charles joined the club, the other members were the John C. Sharp family, the Leverett Saltonstalls, the Frederick L. Ameses, the John H. Sturgises, the Robert Codmans and the William C. Loverings. Year by year this roster would change as families who were to be away for the summer would rent their rooms to friends, only, like all clubs, the unwritten rule was that the name of any new family coming in should be submitted to the other members for approval. Of all the families none was so steadfast in their attendance as the Loverings and the two Adamses, and it is curious and perhaps fitting that the only marriage directly attributable to the Glades was that of Mr. Lovering's daughter Fanny and my brother Charlie, and even that romance took several years to materialize.

The arrival of my father and his brother at the Glades brought a mild revolution in some of the customs. They liberalized the rather rigid Sunday practices, and though services were still held in the public parlors as before, swimming and sailing were no longer frowned on in the afternoons. Later when the transportation question became easier, services were omitted and gradually Sundays turned into a day of social relaxation — with tennis, swimming and sailing — all very pleasant and harmless. The men had long since pre-empted for their exclusive use a spur of rocks at the tip of the point for their swimming pleasure and always before lunch (it was called dinner then) they would troop over there swinging their towels to bathe in comfort and in a state of nature far from any prying eyes at the Glades house. That practice was stopped in World War II as the Naval Station overlooked the Bathing Rocks and was supposed to be out of bounds for civilians — but my stubborn brother Charles could not tolerate having his lifelong habits disrupted by a little thing like a war, and, perhaps with the feeling that having been once a Secretary of the Navy he was entitled to certain privileges, he chose to disregard the ruling, and continued to swim off the rocks under the amused eyes of the naval personnel. As the Bathing Rocks were sacred to the men, the rest of us bathed off an ancient waterlogged wharf moored in front of the house, which was always washed up on the beach by the first hard northeast storm. Occasionally of a chill September morning Uncle Charles would elect to take his customary swim off the wharf, and then if anyone spotted his stocky pink form no mention was made of it, for if they did, Uncle Charles would merely grin wickedly and say, "Well, what did you see?" — Uncle Charles was no prude.

In front of the house and somewhat protected by the outlying rocks known as Gull Ledge and Shephard's there was a fair holding-ground for small boats, and a number were always hanging there. They changed with the current fashion from the cumbersome catboat of earlier times to the sturdy twelve-footers produced by Mr. Herreshoff, and then to the various contraptions of the postwar period. When a northeaster blew in, the holding-ground became dangerous and there was then the great excitement of taking the boats into Cohasset Harbor for safekeeping. It was ticklish work for the small boys to take them in, though perhaps it was good training for some of them who later would be taking in assault waves of landing craft from their ships onto Japanese-held beaches in the Pacific.

Fishing was a disappointment; flounders could be caught off Cohasset, and sometimes a tautog beyond Gull Ledge, but hiring a schooner to go offshore after cod was usually a flop, even with prizes offered for the first and also for the biggest fish, for it was apt to be rough out in the Bay and considerable discomfort might develop among the female sports. Several times a tugboat — usually pretty dirty and smelly — would chug down from Boston to take a party over to Marblehead, twenty miles across the Bay, to follow one of the races at the Eastern Yacht Club in which my brothers George and Charlie were competing. My two elder brothers were, in their way, a rather remarkable pair. George was the older by a couple of years, and had graduated from Harvard with the class of 1886, Charlie following in the class of 1888. George was stocky and square, but though short he played football at Harvard, while Charlie though slight had been an oarsman. George was light-hearted, irresponsible, and convivial but with a never-failing sense of humor, while Charlie was serious-minded, quiet, and absolutely dependable. Though curiously differ-

ent they complemented each other perfectly. Charlie was
the boss and George his most loyal lieutenant. George
had a great respect for his younger brother for all that he
had early nicknamed him "The Deacon" — adding as a
corollary, "The Deacon does not drink" — while Charlie
delighted in George's humor and delicious sense of fun.
Their great mutual interest was in sailing, and they had begun as little boys in Quincy Bay where my old friend, the
inmate of the Sailor's Snug Harbor, Captain Jones, had
given them their first instruction. From then on their interest grew by leaps and bounds fostered by my father's keen-
ness, which was as great as their own, and the fine sailing
opportunities offered by the Glades. By the time that they
were out of college my father had supplied them with a
racing cutter and they were on their way to becoming outstanding yachtsmen. For luck they named their boats with
seven letters and a double *O* — which produced such names
as *Papoose*, *Gossoon*, *Harpoon*, *Rooster*, etc., the names
spelled as suited their fancy. Of course we at the Glades
were wildly enthusiastic over their prowess, and incidentally my father tried to urge me on to become a yachtsman
too. With that end in view an old double-ended cooting
boat, the *Sheldrake*, was turned over to me. She was a
cumbersome boat with an awkward sprit-sail rig, and it
took quite a breeze to take her out of a walk. I did my
best under my father's patient instruction, but I never could
master the proper techniques, and when alone would always prefer to catch the moorings over the stern instead

of luffing up to them properly. One day I learned the hard way by being jerked overboard and nearly drowned before I was picked up by a passing fisherman. That rather discouraged my parents in their belief in my abilities, and with the advent of Mrs. Beach I became a horsewoman instead.

Mrs. Beach was a well-known riding mistress from New York, who was summering at Cohasset one year, and used to come over to the Glades and give us some riding lessons. An old snapshot shows me mounted on a fat amiable carriage horse wearing a shade hat of my mother's and looking positively imbecile with pleasure. The riding lessons were such a success that the following year a riding master from the New Riding Club in Boston — Mr. Spear — used to come down several days a week to take us out. We even set up a hurdle in the hay field on the second point over which we lurched at intervals when the flies were too bad for long rides on the road. All that was before the invasion of the automobile and when the back roads of the pleasant rural hinterland were still soft.

The general tone of the Glades has always been extraordinarily simple, friendly, and democratic. I doubt if a pleasanter example of communal living could anywhere be found — for even with a number of such high-spirited men as my Uncle Charles, Mr. Fred Ames, Mr. Robert Codman, Mr. Leverett Saltonstall, and later Mr. Henry Hunnewell, no serious quarrel ever developed, and though there was plenty of grumbling and complaining, it was never ill-tempered or acrimonious and often in the end was treated with amused humor. The communal dining room made for sociability, for, though each family had its own table, it was the custom after meals, particularly after supper, for everyone to forgather for a little conviviality. We would all sit on one of the piazzas in the most uncomfortable and indestructible of wooden chairs where we would either watch the sunset or discuss endlessly such vital subjects as the distance of the star Arcturus from the earth. I don't remember any political discussions or ever any mention of the stock market. Of course my father was a Cleveland Democrat, and Mr. Lovering was the Republican member of Congress from the Twelfth Massachusetts district, but I believe that it was lack of interest and not tact that kept them off the subject. They simply preferred to tackle minor questions. Of course when the Lizzie Borden case came along in 1892, everyone was agog with theories of all sorts, to say nothing of the Dreyfus affair that followed it. Even these excitements did not prevent my brother Charlie from falling asleep in his chair, a feat that no one else could accomplish, but then Charlie could fall asleep while steering a boat and several times, when moonlight sailing, would quietly run his craft on some familiar rock — and then, half asleep, jump overboard and shove her off again.

With the advent of the Henry Hunnewell family in 1897, the card-playing era began with a vengeance. Mr. Hunnewell was aided and abetted by the Coxes — Mr. Lovering's daughter and son-in-law — the Henry Chapins and the R. M. Saltonstalls, and soon we were all playing like

mad and sleepy evenings on the piazza were relegated to
the older group. Mr. Hunnewell loved games, competition and fun, and his enthusiasm was so infectious that we
all promptly succumbed and the card-playing has gone on
ever since. We started with Russian bezique, to be discarded later for bridge which has long been prime favorite.
With a delicate sense of what might create ill feeling, it was
decreed that we should play for beans and not money and
the happy possessor of the most beans at the end of the
summer should have his or her name engraved on the
Glades Bridge Cup — a nice silver affair much prized and
now quite covered with familiar names. After one lost all
one's beans IOUs were acceptable, and on Labor Day the
beans would be counted and the cup presented to the new
winner by the preceding one. Labor Day was the great
summing up of the season — there was the tennis tour-
nament to be decided, the cup presented, a clambake to be
organized, followed in the evening by a song fest beginning with all the old favorites and ending with some well-
rendered hymns. Christine Hunnewell Bartlett was always
our spirited and indefatigable accompanist and our refreshments varied from Welsh Rarebits while we still enjoyed the
services of a chef, to more plebeian crackers and ginger
ale in later days.

My memories of childhood at the Glades are almost
more vivid than the later ones, for the years did not slip by
so quickly then — and I was for a long time the youngest
person on the place and so perforce had to associate with

girls who were perhaps ten years my seniors. They were very good to me, but I must have been a complete nuisance for them, as I was always tagging along and listening to their conversation, which I found absorbing. My older brothers felt that they owned the Glades and acted accordingly. They would go off into huddles whenever it was a question of going sailing or any other activity and then they would solemnly reappear and announce the plans — who should go in what boat — and then the girls would meekly trot off to change their dresses for whatever sport had been agreed upon. As far as I could see, the girls never questioned Charlie's and George's decision. They accepted their tyranny and paired off just as they were ordered to. After a moonlight sail they were apt to go down to the "dear old kitchen" and try their hand at either grilled sardines or Welsh Rarebit cooked to the accompaniment of the angry buzzing of the infuriated flies. Those expeditions did not include me, so that I only know of them from hearsay.

With my father's death in 1894 and my brother George's in 1900, my recollections become adult ones, for though we continued to pass our summers at the Glades it was never quite the same. My brother Charlie had married, and I had grown up and become one of the older group, while a new generation was beginning to appear. I was married in 1907, but my Glades summers were not interrupted until my mother's death in 1911 when I decided to turn my half share over to my brother Arthur and leave the place for good. My children and I were at Gloucester while my husband was at Camp Devens preparing for war, and later we were at Marblehead when he was overseas, but after he got home and we tried to settle down permanently at Marblehead it did not seem to work out so happily. My son yearned for the Glades where he loved to visit with his cousin young Charlie Adams, and we found that hiring houses every year was a perfect nuisance. So back to the Glades we went, building a house there which we said, rather smugly, might last us while the children were growing up. It has now served us for thirty years — my grandchildren use it now and the end is not yet.

It would be superfluous to try to give a year-by-year list of the Glades families. My sister-in-law Mrs. Charlie Adams (Fanny) used to say that she had lived there for over eighty summers and that no two summers had ever been alike, but though the inhabitants might vary, the background and spirit of the place never did. I like to think that what she said was true. Her older sister Mrs. Henry B. Coxe (Ruth) had been there almost as long, and both sisters were greatly beloved. Mrs. Harry Coxe was a Philadelphian, which helped to mellow the Boston atmosphere. Mrs. Coxe would arrive each year with a trunk full of wool for knitting, a five-pound box of marshmallows to start the season off properly, and a huge bottle of Cascara pills for the benefit of all concerned. Each year she would knit everyone on the place a pair of bedroom slippers after an exclusive pattern of her own — and produce in the course of the summer several mammoth Jack Horner pies, not just for the children but for the entire company, which meant a whole barrelful of presents, and a great deal of laughter.

There have been accidents at the Glades but, thank heaven, nothing serious. Children had their teeth knocked out and their heads cut open but nothing worse. The barn burned down one spring before the place opened, but the wind was offshore so that the house was not involved, no animals were in the barn, and plenty of fire insurance left us all rejoicing. Then later came the 1938 hurricane which, luckily, occurred after we had all left, and though that would have been a good opportunity for the old house to collapse, nothing much happened; a couple of chimneys blew down and a lot of shingles ripped off the roofs, but that was about all.

During the life of the Glades Club two wrecks have occurred, but neither involved loss of life, and curiously enough both happened during the summer months. The first was the bark *Joseph A. Ropes* which in a thick fog one night in 1886 ran onto the Grampus rocks. The Grampuses had been the scene of a hideous wreck nearly forty years before when the immigrant ship *St. John* had gone to pieces there with a very heavy loss of life, and the place was justly feared. The *Ropes* was in no danger and the boys at the Glades at once went out to visit her, taking newspapers and fresh vegetables. They came back with the gruesome story that the Captain's wife had died on the voyage and that her body was in the hold preserved in a cask of rum. The *Ropes* was gotten off without difficulty and was subsequently lost off Madagascar.

The next wreck was more of the comic opera variety, for on a lovely quiet afternoon in 1900 the *John Endicott*, an excursion steamer on her way up from Plymouth, tried a short cut through what we called the Gangway and came to grief. No harm was done, but the excitement at the Glades was intense. What men were at home at the time tried to launch the Humane Society lifeboat, but failing that they took to the water in canoes and paddled out like mad. Their help was not needed but at least they might have been heroes. Ruth Coxe, who among her many talents was a competent watercolorist, immediately sat down and painted a picture of the stranded *Endicott* of which we are justly proud.

During the war years from 1941 to 1945, the United States took over all the Glades property, which they called Strawberry Point, and both the Army and the Navy had a whack at it. We were allowed to live there under certain restrictions such as blackout and having a sentry always stationed at Wattles Beach. He had a little shack below my house and was a great help in relaying messages and sometimes in killing snakes for me. The two services built all sorts of contraptions on the place including gun emplacements, towers for searchlights and for observation, concrete houses to fool the Germans and to conceal electrical equipment, to say nothing of a whole fleet of barracks. The Navy had its own neat little naval station on our highest eminence, which in conjunction with a similar post at Nahant, across the Bay, was supposed to command the approaches to Boston Harbor. With all this defense we never suffered from enemy action, but the zeal of the Navy did manage to kill our one poor old farm horse. He was an independent animal and preferred roaming around at night to being shut up in the barn, only unfortunately when challenged by the sentry he merely shifted his position in the bushes and was shot for his pains. The Navy was most apologetic and we all tried our best to save the poor beast, but one very hot night he lay down and died right under my bedroom window, and as it was very hard to get a knacker to come and remove him, I had a miserable time of it for several days. The officers both of the Army and Navy were very pleasant and got some fun out of our tennis courts when they were not too busy. All this building activity ruined our modest dirt avenue, and the Commonwealth of Massachusetts for the benefit of both services constructed a splendid new road into the place complete with beautiful white guard posts. The State engineers only slipped up when it came to the problem of Wattles Beach, for they brushed aside our well-meant advice as to the idiosyncrasies of that locality and proceeded at vast expense to build a magnificent causeway across the beach — six feet and more above high-water mark. It was a most impressive erection and lasted just one winter. The following year a rip-snorter storm came along and when the sea was finished with our handsome road there was nothing left of it but some odd lumps of concrete, a few battered posts, which we salvaged, and huge yawning holes where the sea had broken through and leveled it all away. As the Navy was then leaving, the State did not see fit to replace the road, so we have gone back to the old conservative method of letting the waves sweep over the road àt their own sweet will hoping that if we don't oppose them they will treat us more gently. Still we realize that we are putting up a losing fight and that the sea will win out in the end leaving the Glades an island.

The Glades has been very lucky all these years and that it still exists is proof not only of its vitality but of its usefulness. As the older members died their descendants have filled the ranks, and somehow the place has carried on through changing times. But if you should go down there when everyone has left you will feel and almost see the ghosts of the older generation — for when the place is empty they come into their own again. I even saw one once but no one will believe me, so I remain silent on the subject.

CHAPTER TEN

I N THE SPRING of 1904 I was planning a visit to Uncle
Henry, which was to be combined with a riding trip up
the Shenandoah Valley with my horsy friend Mrs. Herbert
Wadsworth who had a huge house in Washington. She was
a most unusual and energetic woman who had been my
hostess for several autumns in the Genesee Valley, where
she had not only mounted me for the hunts with the Genesee Valley hounds but given me a wonderful time in

every way. She was not at all Uncle Henry's cup of tea, but he bore it bravely. After all, he liked her husband Herbert Wadsworth, and Herbert's older brother Austen was a friend of Uncle Brooks's.

It was at that time during a tea at the White House that Mrs. Hay (whose husband was now Secretary of State) invited me to go out to the St. Louis Fair with Uncle Henry and themselves. Uncle Henry, she said, was coming to keep Mr. Hay company and I must come to keep Uncle Henry company, while they were doing their official duties. It seemed a large assignment, but of course I accepted just the same. It all worked beautifully for they were not to start until my riding trip was over. The next day, to get broken in, I went to a swank luncheon at the Hays' given in honor of a visiting Chinese prince. President and Mrs. Roosevelt were there; the Cabot Lodges, the Chinese Ambassador and other dignitaries. I couldn't see exactly where I fitted in, but when I asked Uncle Henry for enlightenment he merely said that Mrs. Hay always knew her business best.

Shortly afterwards our Shenandoah trip started — Mr. and Mrs. Wadsworth (he rather reluctantly), Percy Wyndham of the British legation and a delightful Hungarian named Zichy. We were gone a week, saw the Shenandoah Valley at its best and came home by the Luray Caverns in Virginia. In the few days that I then had in Washington, I remember Uncle Henry taking me over to tea at the White House with the President and Mrs. Roosevelt, where, perhaps in consideration of Uncle Henry's diffidence, we were

the only visitors. That was one of the occasions outside of
his own house where Uncle Henry was at his best, for Mrs.
Roosevelt could keep the President from barging into the
conversation. Uncle Henry did not like to be interrupted,
but the President loved to talk and the temptation was
sometimes irresistible unless Mrs. Roosevelt was on hand
to control him.

The St. Louis trip was for me the greatest fun. I had
never traveled by private car (we had the one belonging
to the Cassatts of the Pennsylvania Railroad) with V.I.P.'s
and I adored it — the nice colored attendants, the privacy
and the comfort. It was blissful. The fair was quite flat in
comparison to the trip out, for I had been to fairs before.
Mr. and Mrs. Hay were received with the proper cere-
monies and Uncle Henry and I tagged along as incon-
spicuously as possible, so much so that we were usually
completely ignored, and saw the fair on our own. Uncle
Henry was thrilled by the dynamos and suchlike, but in a
lighter vein we sampled all the restaurants, and had several
good laughs over the art exhibitions. How Uncle Henry
stood it I don't know, but I had a lovely time and laughed

a good deal over his sallies at the modern world. One of the few expeditions on which we were part of the official party was a river trip up the Mississippi to where the Missouri flows into it. It wasn't a particularly interesting sight, but we had a band on board which kept up a vigorous tootling when someone or other was not busy making a speech, and there were also tons of food on board — enough to satisfy all hands.

It was not many years after that that I was married; and while engaged I took my fiancé, Robert Homans, down to Washington to be inspected by Uncle Henry. Bob was the son of an old college friend of his, Dr. John Homans of Boston, and Uncle Henry approved of Bob at first sight and was amused and interested by his lively intelligence and sense of humor. My fiancé was a lawyer by trade and had been in Washington as a secretary of Mr. Justice Gray of the Supreme Court — which was all to the good. As we left, Uncle Henry said, "Well, infants, when you are fed up with your honeymoon come and see me in Paris." Since we were planning a European trip, his suggestion fitted into our itinerary perfectly. We sailed from Boston, and Mr. Justice Holmes of the Supreme Court was also on board. As he was an old family friend and as I was a young woman (and he liked young women), he talked to me every day on the voyage over. My husband was naturally flattered at his attentions to me and asked me what we had been talking about all the time. I said, quite truthfully, that the Justice had done most of the talking and

that it was all about the "ultimate cosmos" and that I still
didn't know what it was. Bob was delighted. After we
landed at Liverpool we all went up together in the train to
London, and the last I saw of the Justice he was all dolled
up in evening clothes looking splendidly distinguished and
handsome en route to dinner with a duchess.

We stayed only a few weeks in England, but long
enough to take in Henley with some American friends and
have Bob come to grief while trying his hand at poling a
punt after lunching with Lady Astor at Cliveden. Paris
was our next stop and a call on Uncle Henry at his apartment was the key to a lovely adventure. Luckily we found
him at rather loose ends; his friends had all left and he was
delighted to have us fill in his time. We lunched or dined
with him — often both — almost every day. He took us
to the most fashionable restaurants and always ordered a
bottle of champagne. It was great fun. He took us several
times to the theater but not to the Comédie Française. On
the contrary, and rather to my surprise, we were taken
to some funny but very indecent farces. They usually
shocked me, and Uncle Henry would laugh when he saw
my prim little puckered-up face and say, "It's a far cry from
Quincy, Mass." My husband, though he took the French
vulgarity much more serenely than I did — he may even
have enjoyed it — was bothered by Uncle Henry's one-
sided hospitality, and ventured one evening to suggest that
he might dine with us the following day. "Oh," laughed
Uncle Henry, "don't bother your head about that, my dear

fellow, you are only eating on my heirs," and that was the last word on that score.

Of all our jaunts together the best was when we spent a day at Chartres under Uncle Henry's guidance. There he seemed to wear the mantle of a prophet, and we certainly accepted him as such. He had a marvelous faculty as a teacher, and once he realized that we were really ardently interested he let himself go and became positively loquacious in his eagerness to impart something of his own enthusiasm. To us hidebound New Englanders it was almost like a revelation, and made the whole experience supreme. We sat under the stained-glass windows while he explained the stories, and then watched the afternoon light set the Tree of Jesse ablaze.

Shortly afterwards we left Paris, but Uncle Henry instructed us to see Mont St. Michel and not to miss Autun and Vézelay. At Autun he told us to notice one of the most naïve and charming of the carved Romanesque capitals, the capital of the magi, where the three kings are in bed together, one of them being awakened by an angel. The other thing that he said was a "must" was the tympanum at Vézelay. But by that time we had become regular bird dogs over capitals and tympanums and could smell the thirteenth century a mile off.

CHAPTER ELEVEN

THE FEW YEARS after my marriage were not so fruit-
ful in visits to Uncle Henry. My husband was busy
with his law practice, and after a while I too had domestic
duties to tie me down. Still we managed to get down to
Washington each winter, though our visits were only of
the over-Sunday variety. Uncle Henry remained much the
same, though he missed John Hay, who had died in 1905,
and had substituted a daily drive for the afternoon constitu-

tional which the two had always taken together. In 1912 Uncle Henry had a stroke, but it was not a very severe one, and for that summer his brother Charles took charge of him and established him in a small house near his own in South Lincoln, where he made an astonishing recovery. The next year he went abroad as usual, but the European war that he had long predicted finally caught up with him. He contrived to leave France and take refuge in his friend Mrs. Cameron's house in Dorset before coming home for good.

With France no longer available for his annual expeditions, he became dependent on what his own country could offer him in the way of summer sanctuaries. One year he went to Dublin, New Hampshire, and the next to the Berkshires. There in 1916 we found him ensconced in a magnificent mansion at Tyringham where we made him a long over-Sunday visit. It was a huge house built by Mrs. Robb de Peyster Titus, a gifted and brilliant woman. The house was a tribute to her artistic qualities, a truly splendid achievement, built on a steep wooded hillside and commanding a stupendous view to the west. The interior was as grand as old paneling and period furniture could make it. I slept in a gorgeous canopied bed quite unsuited to hot August nights and unpleasantly suggestive of ghosts. Dr. Sturgis Bigelow was also a guest, and Miss Aileen Tone as well. In fact, Uncle Henry seemed very happily situated, amused by his mock medieval habitation and delighted at the idea of himself as a modern robber baron in the wilds

of Massachusetts. The usual occupation of Uncle Henry
was motoring around the charming, unspoiled countryside,
but for us in search of exercise, this did not fill the bill. We
made an intensive search for Mr. Titus's grave, supposed
to be somewhere in the neighboring hills, but we never
found it, possibly because the prevalence of snakes in the
vicinity was too much for my feeble nerves.

The following year, 1917, Uncle Henry was in his own
house in Beverly Farms, where I think he was contented,
for all that it was full of sad memories of his early married
years. This was one of the summers we spent away from
the Glades, and were living in nearby Gloucester. I went
down several times to lunch with Uncle Henry, taking my
young son with me, as it was a wonderful opportunity for
him to meet his great-uncle. It was fortunate that I did, for
the next spring Uncle Henry died. He died just as he had
hoped to, quietly in his sleep, and he was buried in Washington beside his wife, under the St. Gaudens figure that he
had commissioned for her.

My father had died in 1894, Uncle Charles in 1915, and
now Uncle Henry's death left Uncle Brooks the last sur-
vivor of the four brothers. I had always seen a great deal of
him in Quincy, especially after his marriage, when he
moved there permanently. He had a house in Boston for
the winter months, but he loved the Old House and the
garden beside it and he was disturbed over what would become of the place at his death. None of the descendants
wanted to live there, as Quincy was no longer a pleasant

country retreat, while the house itself, for all its historic interest, was inconvenient and old-fashioned according to modern standards. To Uncle Brooks, none of that mattered. He was very proud of the garden which he had restored according to John Adams's original plan, while the house was endeared to him by all the family relics and memorabilia. Each generation had left the house as they had found it, so that, though it was neither beautiful nor elegant, it had interest and charm. Uncle Henry had never removed his share of the portraits when they were divided among the brothers, so the dining room still had the portraits of George and Martha Washington by Savage which had been a gift of the Washingtons to the John Adamses. As the bill for them was still pasted on the back of one, I have always wondered which family paid.

Not only was Uncle Brooks fond of me, but to my great surprise he became much attached to my husband. I had warned Bob, as I have said, that it was essential for him to at least get on pleasantly with Uncle Brooks, so he agreed that he would do his best, and kept murmuring to himself, "Remember to like Mr. Adams." As a matter of fact, it all worked out beautifully. Uncle Brooks responded quickly to sympathy and appreciation and was pleased by Bob's friendly approach. One result was the trip I have mentioned up to Plattsburg, New York, where Bob was in the Officers' Training Camp in the war summer of 1918, which led to Uncle Brooks's annoying letter telling me that I didn't half appreciate my husband! Was I mad when I received that message!

Later when the war was over, Uncle Brooks got Bob to form the Adams Memorial Society to protect the Old House and its contents. It was made up of the remaining descendants of John and Abigail Adams, and was to hold and administer the Old House forever. The Society functioned efficiently and, after Uncle Brooks's death in 1927, opened the house to the public until 1946, when it was presented to the Government and became a National Historic Site, since which it has been beautifully cared for by the Department of the Interior.

As to the disposition of the family relics: the Manuscript Trust had been instituted in 1905 after long and often heated discussion by the brothers. It had been for years an open question as to what could be done with the huge accumulation of books and papers collected by their forebears. There were not only diaries and letters, but miscellaneous documents, many of great interest to scholars and historians. When the Old House was bursting at its seams, in the seventies, the Stone Library in the garden was built to house the masses of books and the family manuscripts, but when it was pointed out that the library was not fireproof, the vexed frustration of the family raised its head once again. Before my father's death in 1894 I remember being present at a meeting with him and his brothers Charles and Brooks in regard to the papers. The discussion seemed interminable and my father at last losing patience said, "Come on, Charles, let's burn the d—— things." He was undoubtedly talking from exasperation or just in a spirit of mischief, but the threat did the trick. Shortly afterwards the brothers decided — pusillanimously — to simply shut the papers up and let them lie fallow for fifty years more.

As Uncle Charles pointed out, "We shall all be dead by then and the next generation can take the responsibility." The truth is that the brothers were a little afraid of the papers. No one had been through them all and there were dark hints that they held some unpleasant scandals, so they washed their hands of the whole affair. The next generation had no such qualms and, scandals or not, in 1954 de-

cided to allow the papers, which had long since been placed
for safekeeping in a locked room at the Massachusetts Historical Society, to be opened for scholarly use. A microfilm
edition was begun by the Historical Society in 1952 and
completed in 1959. In the meantime, the Harvard University Press expressed keen interest in publishing the Papers. Lyman Butterfield, then director of the Institute of
Early American History and Culture at Williamsburg, Virginia, was placed in charge of this enterprise, with financial
support from Time, Inc. on behalf of *Life*, which was to
print selections in its columns. Later, after a number of vol-
umes had appeared and it became clear that perhaps a hundred would be needed to complete *The Adams Papers*, the
Ford Foundation gave further financial aid.

Uncle Brooks would have been satisfied, if, when he died
in 1927, he could have known that his beloved relics were
at last to be in safe hands.